TOGETHER WE SERVE

Four Proven Strategies to Create Winning Experiences for Your Guests and Your Team

Tony Johnson, CCXP

TOGETHER WE SERVE

Four Proven Strategies to Create
Winning Experiences
for Your Guests and Your Team

Written by
TONY JOHNSON

*"Often the difference between winning and losing is
the determination and grit to bring ideas to life."*
-TONY JOHNSON-

Published By
THE TONY JOHNSON, LLC
WWW.THETONYJOHNSON.COM

Published by

TheTonyJohnson, LLC
THETONYJOHNSON.COM

Printed in the United States of America

Cover Design by Julia Mezo

ISBN: 978-0-578-47738-1

Disclaimer:

The purpose of this book is entertainment and education. The author and publisher shall have neither liability nor responsibility for anyone with respect to any loss or damage caused, directly or indirectly, by the information contained in this book. While every effort was made to verify information contained within this publication, neither the author nor publisher assumes any responsibility for errors, omissions, or inaccuracies. This publication is not intended to provide legal, financial, or business advice. The author and publisher assume no responsibility or liability in an way or whatsoever on the behalf of the reader of this publication.

Acknowledgements

I WOULD LIKE to thank the following, whose support was invaluable and made this book possible.

Thank you to all who serve, who serve those who serve, and who believe in the power of service.

To Tom Johnson and Alice Johnson, the parents who instilled in me empathy and a sense of hard work.

To my sister Kristine, who was always one of my biggest supporters.

To Shaun and Jenny Slade, thank you for being such amazing friends.

To Makayla and Katelyn, my amazing nieces who remind me to look at things from a child's point of view and remember that it all begins with fun. To Ben, I am always proud of you beyond words.

To my Aunt Reta, who was always like a second mom.

To Geno Svec, Mario Toussaint, Shawn Simpson, and Clint Westbrook, you are the most amazing sounding boards who never hold back and always encourage.

To Scott and Amanda Bauerschmidt, many thanks for the fun and laughs between writing stints.

To Michelle, Mike, Josh, Linsday, Sue, Angie, and Tom for all of your love and support.

I also want to thank the teams I have worked with over the years. To all of you, thank you for making me a better leader and teaching me that you can't take care of guests without taking great care of the team who serves them. I'm humbled by your service.

Thank you to the CXPA for your continuing professionalism and dedication to the guest experience.

Finally, and most importantly, to my wife Melissa. Thank you for all the love and support you have given me over the last decade. You have inspired me, leveled with me, and been the most amazing muse. I couldn't have written this without you.

Tony

Let's work together to deliver the
best possible experiences to your guests.

Beyond the pages of this book are a wealth of resources
to help you train your team, establish accountability,
and sustain your service culture.

We are open 24 x 7 at:
WWW.IGNITEYOURSERVICE.COM

Feel free to reach out to me or my team directly:

Tony@igniteyourservice.com

Melissa@igniteyourservice.com

I am also available to speak to your group or organization.
If you need a high energy trainer or keynote
for your next event, meeting, or conference,
reach out directly to:

info@igniteyourservice.com

**Dates book fast, so please call TODAY to add
Motivation, Customer Focus,
and High Energy to your Event!**

Tony Johnson, CCXP

Facebook: /TonyJohnsonCX

Twitter: @ServiceRecipe

Snapchat: thetonyjohnson

Instagram: @recipeforservice

TOGETHER WE SERVE

Four Proven Strategies to Create Winning Experiences for Your Guests and Your Team

Contents

EXECUTIONAL SUCCESS

SERVICE SUCCESS

Introduction

Let's start our journey together

IF YOU ARE reading this, we are on the journey together already.

Thanks for joining in and let's make the most of our time together.

First, remember that words have meaning, but your actions matter more. I believe deep down that we all serve guests. Whether you work in retail, hospitality, restaurants, hotels, theme parks, hospitals, or in education, you serve guests. The sooner we all recognize this the better off our guests will be.

You may see me use the words guest, customer, and consumer throughout this book, but what matters most is the sentiment behind it. What matters is the way you treat people who visit your business or use your services. You may be in a consumer business, such as beverages, electronics, or online commerce, but don't let the word consumer become antiseptic and without feeling. There is always someone on the other end of the process who is depending on you to get it right, so keep people in mind no matter what you do. I use those words to connect with the various segments that can find success with these strategies and tactics, but you must never forget the personal touch.

Your guests, customers, or consumers are the ones who will benefit from your product or service. They cannot be faceless statistics but rather the mothers who will use the sunscreen on their children or the business travelers who depends on your suitcases to roll easily when they arrive home on a 1 a.m. flight.

You have the power as a leader to set the tone for your group, and if you are a department of one or work directly on the front line, you have the power to deliver that service directly. Regardless of where you work in an organization, you can set a good example and inspire greatness.

The more you can work the word guest into your vernacular the more apt everyone around you is to pick up that phraseology as well. And if you begin by calling people guests, it does help drive the actions that make it more than just words.

Finally, leaders, please lead. Please lead with enthusiasm and candor and authenticity. Show your team your passion and don't be afraid to let them get to know you a bit.

When I think about leadership, it is more about the ability to influence your team, your organization, and even your supervisors. Leadership isn't always about your position in the organization, but rather how you model behaviors and share your passion for service. You don't need to be the CEO or even a high-level executive to improve guest service – more important is the impact you bring to the guest in front of you. Service is less about strategic planning and more about the thousands of small interactions you have with guests along the way.

You will find themes that are reinforced throughout the book – empathy, listening, looking at things from the guest point of view – this is by design as these are themes that we cannot over-discuss. You will see how these pieces recur as we discuss methods for success and illustrate their importance in various actions to turn service to experience and your company into a brand. Nothing happens in a silo, it all interconnects and overlaps.

Nothing happens without action and passion – you can't move an apple cart or a mountain without them. So, keep in mind that there will be some "what" in this book but mostly a whole lot of "how." And a big part of that "how" is to take the principles and key moves we discuss and do something with them. Don't skip the action nuggets at the end of each chapter, but don't just read them and think you're getting the whole story either.

I've spent decades serving guests and leading teams and the pages that follow are a culmination of how I have been able to move organizations of dozens, hundreds, and thousands over the years to put guests center stage, driving satisfaction, loyalty, and repeat business.

1

....

TOGETHER WE SERVE

Service is a team sport.

NOTHING REALLY GREAT happens alone. It takes a team to bring it to life.

Service has always come very naturally to me. I believe that the noblest thing we can do is to be of service to each other.

I love taking care of people and it has always been something that gives me great joy and pride.

But that doesn't mean it's always easy. It can be frustrating – damned frustrating. But that doesn't mean it isn't worth it either.

Service is tough stuff. It means that you have to put other's needs above your own and go to market each day looking to make people's lives better. That is why it not only takes a personal commitment to excellence, but a team to bring it to life.

I am reminded of what teamwork looks like every time I see an airline captain leave the flight deck. Ever since 911, there are very prescriptive processes with regard to the security of the cockpit. If you get a chance to watch this security ballet, you'll smile at the level of teamwork and orchestration it takes. It begins with the "bing" that lets the flight attendants know that one of the flight crew will be exiting. Then comes the beverage cart wedged in to block the path into the flight deck. Finally, the door opens and out comes the captain and in goes a flight attendant. The process is then reversed, and everyone is back in position. This maneuver has many moving pieces and processes that must be executed for it to happen safely and without drawing too much attention. It happens as a matter of course. Effortless and nonchalant, but effective all the same.

I mention this story because it shows the importance of teamwork – in this case the protection and safety of both the passengers and the crew. But teamwork matters when it comes to delivering top notch execution and service to guests too. Now this may seem like one of those "well, yeah" kind of moments, but it's worth talking about because as I spend time with teams in all sorts of industries – from restaurants to colleges to banking – everyone talks about the importance (and lack) of teamwork.

It has almost become cliché to hear about teamwork in planning meetings and employee opinion surveys, but that's because we are fundamentally flawed at providing it.

> *This is where you need to gut check yourself and your organization for what kind of culture you are reinforcing. Teamwork starts at the senior level of most organizations and that means setting a tone where teamwork is embraced.*

This is where you need to gut check yourself and your organization for what kind of culture you are reinforcing. Teamwork starts at the senior level of most organizations and that means setting a tone where teamwork is embraced. Sure, it is nice to revere the individual contributions, but you can't let the quest for individual achievement turn your organization into a ruthless competition for credit.

Now, the flip side is that you can benefit from a little healthy competition to drive results. It doesn't have to be mean spirited or intense, but just enough to keep folks from becoming lackadaisical.

Whether you are a leader or a department of one, people are what make great service happen. It takes leadership to inspire a team to provide great service and the team to provide the day to day muscle to make it happen. This book will provide leadership strategies to drive change along with the tactical steps needed to provide service directly to guests. It has applicability within every level of any organization that seeks to improve the experience of its guests.

If you are a manager or supervisor, you will find strategies in here to inspire and lead your team.

If you serve guests directly, you will find relevant tactics in here to care for guests on the front line of service.

Never doubt the part you play individually and collectively within your organization to change your guests' days for the better.

Because together we serve.

TAKE ACTION:

At the end of each chapter we will discuss key actions you can take to drive success with what we discussed in the preceding pages. Take the time to review and note how you can make an impact using the steps outlined.

Remember, reading this book and having great intentions will have very little impact on your leadership or your organization if you don't take the time to craft a plan.

Sometimes you'll have to make notes, other times they will just be reminders or next steps, but you'll always need to take action.

Leadership is about engagement, so take the time at the end of each chapter to consider what you're your next steps will be and capture them while they are still fresh.

- Great service doesn't happen alone. What are departments or groups responsible for in each part of your guest experience?

- What is your current service culture? Do you have one?

- How can you leverage a little healthy competition to get everyone engaged in great execution and service

2

. . . .

BUILDING THE FOUNDATION

The foundational four that we will build upon

THIS BOOK IS broken down into four foundational elements that every business needs to adopt regardless of discipline or size: Team Success, Leadership Success, Executional Success, and Service Success.

So many leaders start by thinking about quality and execution, and I understand the allure of focusing on execution. But let's reset how we think about business execution and go back to the fundamental elements that make up great execution. Rarely does execution exist in a vacuum without being the product of a human factor.

While it's easy to say blithely that service is all about people – understanding it is another thing all together.

There are four core principles that we will be covering in this book. With these you'll find that each of the chapters in the section support the ideas and help you bring them to life.

Taking action and driving results is where there is sometimes a disconnect between knowledge and activity. That is where those who really excel do things a little differently.

Think about the basic example of listening. Most everyone knows how to be a good listener, but somewhere along the way they either forgot or chose not to activate the key moves. You can choose to let the other person talk, stay focused on what they are saying, and not interrupt – but how many of us have the force of will to do so?

Not many.

Most folks are terrible listeners because they choose to be, not because they don't know how.

So that is the theme you will find throughout this book. You may find nuggets that make you think and those that teach you something new, and along the way there will be things you read that you may consider common knowledge.

That is where you will need to dig in. This is where you will need to apply yourself. Don't dismiss it as not worth your time, but rather ask yourself if you are executing those key moves. Everything mentioned within these pages is done so intentionally – and usually because it helps me drive success when leading teams and delighting guests.

> *Customer service comes from people. It is led by people, consumed by people, and leads to the success of people. When we think foundationally about how we grow, accelerate, and sustain a culture of service it becomes clear that we have to consider the following four fundamental pillars.*

Customer service comes from people. It is led by people, consumed by people, and leads to the success of people. When we think foundationally about how we grow, accelerate, and sustain a culture of service it becomes clear that we have to consider the following four fundamental pillars. Everything that we hope to create within an organization comes back to these core elements.

These are worth noting because everyone in the organization must be aligned to the needs of guests and consumers, as well as those who serve them. Customer service isn't limited to any one group and the future of creating great experiences for guests is about complete organizational alignment. Everyone has to be involved and understand their impact on service.

When organizations talk about building culture it must begin by ensuring that every team member is involved in designing and delivering great experiences. That starts by keeping the customer in mind at every turn and understanding they are the focal point of every effort. Departments who begin without considering the impact on guests and those who deliver services to them will find that their efforts, while likely earnest, will fall flat.

Consider these four fundamental pillars to driving a service culture:

- **Team Success**
- **Leadership Success**
- **Executional Success**
- **Service Success**

Let's dig in a little on each of these.

Team Success:

This is where excellence begins. It starts with the team you lead to serve your guests and the care your team is given. Think about it like this: how you treat your team is how they will treat your guests. Your team is the closest part of your organization to the guest and they are the ones who will be seen as the face of your organization.

That is why you must think about the overall employee experience in concert with your goals for the guest experience. This means that not only do you need to consider the experience of your guests but also of the teams who serve them.

Leadership Success:

This all stems from the leaders who serve their teams. It goes without saying that you need to either be serving customers or taking care of those who serve customers. People love to talk about servant leadership, taking care of their team, and leaders who ask the right questions. The problem here is that it's just lip service. I have spent the last year talking to front line associates in many disciplines and industries, and their core issue is that their leaders are MIA. Their leaders don't listen. Their leaders are absent when they are needed and not engaged when they are involved. Leaders make decisions without consultation, explanation, or follow up. Without context, decisions appear to have been made in a vacuum and as a result the front-line teams believe that "management doesn't know what's going on." The idea of leadership making decisions without considering the team may have gone out of fashion years ago, but that is not always the reality. Even though it is counterproductive to engagement, and not ideal for the guest experience, teams continue to operate this way.

To turn the page and drive success, leaders must lead differently. They have to lead with the vision that sets the stage for success and helps craft the way forward. A collaborative process that breeds inclusion and a sense of purpose for those who own front-line guest interactions is needed.

Executional Success:

Without great execution, service is just nice people doing a bad job. We all know places like this – all promises and no results. When we consider the whole guest experience, it is clear that execution is a key part of this. So, consider that everything from the quality of the product to the cleanliness of the business is a part of the overall guest experience. We will talk more later about the journey your guest and consumers take when doing business with you, but the key thing to remember here is that it isn't just about providing great service, it is about considering how everything that your guests interact with impacts their satisfaction and their ease of use. Now lots of people like to talk about effortless experiences and simple business models - almost to the point of over-simplification. I think it's more important to think about making things as easy as possible and as simple as possible. I've spent a career listening to people talk about wanting a hospitality strategy that fits on a postage stamp – but that's not possible for something as important as service. Don't overcomplicate it, but ensure you have all the tools necessary to fuel success. It's about balance.

Consider execution as the sum of quality, value, and ease.

Quality: Does your product or service meet your guests' expectations. Quality is about the perception of those you serve and the execution of your team. There are several facets to consider here – it could be the product you offer or the combination of your product in conjunction with the service and setting of your business. Quality is often subjective, so ensuring that you have marketed your product properly and then delivered on that commitment is important as well. Some other pieces that impact quality could be speed of service, product knowledge, and support following the sale if assistance is needed.

Value: Do your customers really understand the value you bring, and can you articulate that to them easily? Is your product worth the price and effort? Do they know the difference between you and your competition and does your team understand that difference as well? Yours doesn't need to be the cheapest, it just has to have real value for your guests. Think about tacos. Different people find different value in tacos. Do you believe that value is a $1 taco from a Taco Bell or a Del Taco type of place or would you rather pay a premium for a Qdoba or Chipotle style? The trick here is that each business knows their lane and customer base then caters to their nuances.

Ease: Is it easy to do business with you? That is the ultimate question to consider when you think about your value proposition to guests. When it comes to ease it is all about friction and how easy you make the sales process for your team. Friction occurs when complications are introduced into the service equation and often that can lead to customers leaving your business. Simply put this is when things overwhelm or aggravate your guests to the point when they jump ship on the transaction and head to your competitor.

Service Success:

You are probably thinking to yourself "wait a minute, why isn't service success first?" The rationale is simple. If you don't take care of the three items that proceed this, then you'll never get to a state of perpetual customer success. Many organizations cut right to the guest experience without considering all the prework that has to be completed for great service to be possible. It isn't enough to plant your flag and crow about service, expecting every-

thing to line up. There is work to be done to get there.
Have you selected a team that has a passion for service?
Do your training and engagement strategies lead to a
work force that is enabled and empowered to deliver on
your promise of great service? Consider all of these when
it comes to creating a culture that puts your customers at
the very center of everything you do.

So, the coming chapters will be organized in a way
that helps frame up how to drive team, leadership, execution, and service success. These concepts are nothing
without deeper discussion of the principles that fuel them
and the real-life tactics you can use to bring them to life.
At the end of each chapter you'll find your call to action
that should drive your next steps.

I will tell you that after spending two decades improving the guest experience, growing leaders, and improving performance, it is more about the "how" than the
"what" when it comes to building culture. Chances are
you know much about "what" must be done, but when
you translate that into who will do it, how will it get done,
and when will it happen, that's when you'll find that
things improve.

This is where you have a decision to make, though.
The concepts and principles that will be lined out in the
coming pages are a road map for success in delivering
great service. Together you and your team can serve and
win when it comes to delighting your guests. But, that
means commitment and a refusal to just be okay. You
have to commit to do the hard things that no one else
will. That is the last 10 yards that few will traverse and
where you can set yourself apart.

You will have to make sure your team is trained and equipped when budgets are tight. You can't just throw your hands up and say it can't be done because you don't have the resources.

You have to control what is controllable. Fretting and gnashing about those items that you can't impact right now will do nothing but aggravate you and lead to excuse mongering.

You have to listen to your team and hear their suggestions even when you are exhausted and even if you think you know better.

You have to be honest and clear about your expectations when it comes to quality and service. There can be no ambiguity about what matters most.

You have to be prepared to manage performance in a way that will be uncomfortable. You will need to reward and celebrate those who are delivering and coach those who are not. And then, you will need to be willing to take the uncomfortable step of parting company with those who don't improve.

If you are prepared to take action on these items and really own them, then stay tuned for the critical moves that can help you improve the service in your organization.

TAKE ACTION:

Don't jump straight to execution – think about all the steps that lead up to great experiences. You have to have an engaged and empowered team, leaders who inspire results, and crystal clear standards.

- Does your team understand their roles and their impact on quality?

- If not, how will you communicate this?

- Does your team have the tools and training to do their jobs?

- What gaps need to be filled and how will you do it?

- Do you know what makes up success for your customers?

- If you don't know your customers key wants and needs, engage them to find out.

3

. . . .

THE SIX CANONS RELOADED

The basics never go out of style.

THE CORNERSTONE OF my first book and many of my speaking engagements were the Six Canons of Customer Service. I still use these every day when I speak to groups and organizations about igniting their service, so let's brush them off and talk about why they will always matter.

THE SIX CANONS OF CUSTOMER SERVICE:

1. Smile and Welcome Your Customer Warmly
2. Practice Fantastic Body Language
3. Treat Your Guest as a Cherished Friend
4. Stay Positive and Friendly
5. Make it Easy
6. Thank Every Guest

Here is a spin we'll be looking at this time around –

these are relevant for your internal customers, too.

Think about that. We mentioned earlier that how you treat your team is how they will treat their guests. So, it stands to reason that turning this philosophy inward upon your team is a powerful way to start this chain of success.

So perhaps you don't directly serve customers, which means you are supporting those who do. Indirectly you have the power to drive a great customer experience by assisting those who are delivering services on the front lines. If you are a finance professional, you make sure that the P&L statements are completed and that costs are in line – and help your business stay financially viable. You point out potential inefficiencies and help spot mistakes or opportunities. You may train others to understand how the financials work and thus free them up to think about serving guests (and at the same time do so profitably).

If you are a Human Resources Partner, you may help with selection, training, and recognition. You may create reward programs for high performers and help track performance appraisals. These are core to the mission of service and support those on the front line. You may be equipping leaders to better inspire their teams or making the lives of the front-line associates better.

This is why The Six Canons matter. They not only help to drive success with guests directly, but also to serve those you support or lead each day.

> *The Six Canons came about from decades of leading teams and serving guests in organizations – they are the cornerstone of great service and a solid place to start when you are driving for alignment within your business.*

The Six Canons came about from decades of leading teams and serving guests in organizations – they are the cornerstone of great service and a solid place to start when you are driving for alignment within your business. These are a great way to ground our philosophies of service in tactical moves that can drive success and loyalty. These come in handy if you serve internal and external customers. They also come in handy if you are leading teams and ensuring organizational execution around service strategies.

Later we will talk about a concrete guest engagement framework you can use and teach your teams, but for right now, let's queue up The Six Canons and reload them. You may be wondering what a guest engagement framework is all about – it is a simple step by step structure that helps teams serve guests. When a guest walks up to your counter, enters your office, calls your business, or walks into your store, this is how you take care of them. These will be the very tactical steps that you can use to serve guests.

The Six Canons is the strategy behind them.

Smile and Welcome Your Customer Warmly:

This is, at its core, about making people feel welcomed and comfortable. Guests will return where they feel at home and valued, which all begins with fantastic first impressions. This is fueled by a warm smile, and prompt and sincere greeting.

Many organizations look to high powered strategies to drive guest satisfaction, but here is a small, tactical move that if you can embed in your cultural lexicon, you'll find true movement in guest loyalty.

This is a very situational thing, though.

Depending on your line of work you may deal with folks who are having fantastic day or one of their worst. Think about the difference between someone working at a car dealership helping someone buy their first car and the doctor who may have to deliver terrible news.

These are very different experiences. It is all about measuring the mood in whatever room you may be in and adjusting accordingly – strive to keep your energy one octave above your guest's energy.

Smile and the person across from you will smile back. Its human nature. So, in the world of leading and serving people, it is one of your greatest assets. There is something about a smile that puts people at ease and makes you seem trustworthy. Now those smiles have to be appropriate to be sure, so keep in mind where you are when you flash that great smile. For example, a large and energetic smile may have its place if you are serving someone in a restaurant, but in a hospital, you may need to tone that down to a more subdued version.

The welcome is a tandem partner with a warm smile. There is something about having a fantastic start to a conversation that sets the stage for the rest of the interaction. Plus, when you think about a warm smile and sincere greeting, it makes it less transactional. Any business can have a transaction or sell a product but providing a genuine moment of human connection is something that can set you apart.

Also remember that the welcome is about making sure your guests feel valued. You can do that by ensuring a quick acknowledgement when guests stop by. If you've ever visited a retail establishment and been ignored by the sales team because they were doing something they thought was more important, you can understand this. Guests don't necessarily demand to be served immediately, but they do want a recognition within a few seconds of entering a store or when walking up to a service counter. That may mean saying hello and letting them know that someone will be with them in a moment, but it beats the vacant stare of a busy associate who ignores the guest in front of them because they are settling a cash drawer or washing their hands. There is no sin in saying "Hi, how are you? I'm just finishing this thing and I'll be right with you." And then, don't forget that it's okay to chat with them while you finish whatever that thing is (but do so quickly and serve your guest promptly).

Practice Fantastic Body Language:

Guests are judging us constantly and that means we must always consider ourselves "on stage." I was at a local market a few weeks ago and as I approached the checkout I noticed that the cashier was disheveled, leaning on the cash register, and had a very sour look on her face. I imagine she could have been a very nice, conscientious, and efficient cashier, but I'll be honest, I didn't take the chance. I looked up and down the checkout aisles and picked someone who looked more service oriented. Now this is a definite jerk move on my part, but if we are honest, many of you would have made the same call. Guests will take the path of least resistance and that means making choices with the most upside. For me, that was choosing a cashier that I thought had better odds of providing a fast and friendly service experience.

That means that every nonverbal cue matters – and we are like divining rods when it comes to reading other people. Most of this happens at an unconscious level but that doesn't mean that we don't register it without realizing it. That's why our body language, and the body language of our teams, matters so very much.

The good news is that this is easily understood, and the cues easily trained. But, then it takes diligence during your daily walks through your business to make sure you reinforce these simple key moves.

Body language is about awareness and confidence, so start by ensuring that your team is well trained. More on that in later chapters. You must also ensure that your teams know what proper body language looks like and that they are trained on the following core points:

- **Standing up straight:** No one likes a sloucher or someone leaning all over a counter, cash register, or wall.

- **Kind Eye Contact:** It's not a staring contest but it's also not about looking everywhere but your guest's face. People innately trust folks who make soft eye contact and don't have the appearance of a shifty loan shark.

- **Friendly Smile:** As we discussed earlier, smiles are the secret service weapon. Use them.

- **No Phones, No Gum, No Nonsense:** I remember when you would never have to coach folks to stay off of the phone, but with our current technology addiction you have to be clear that no phones or smart watches should be used while serving guests. Also, when was the last time that someone chomping on gum made a good first impression on you? So, make sure that folks lose the Bubblicious® before stepping on stage to serve guests.

- **Feet Planted and Pointed:** When you keep your feet still and pointed toward guests, you'll find that centers the conversation. When you see folks with their feet pointed away from their conversation partner, it is a signal that they are trying to get away. By staying centered up on the person you are talking to, it shows them that they have your full attention.

- **Arms Wide Open:** Don't cross your arms and coach your team to do the same. This makes you look cut off and unapproachable. This posture will help you seem more open and courteous whether you are speaking with guests or those you work with.

- **Point with Courtesy:** Always remember that pointing with one finger is seen as rude in some cultures. According to Trip Savvy, its most rude in China, Japan, Indonesia, and Latin America. Use a full hand or two finger point if you want to avoid issues – or walk your guest to the place they are seeking and really knock it out of the park.

The final point when it comes to body language is it's important to be confident. When you and your team stand up straight with your arms uncrossed you exude a certain kind of approachable confidence.

Treat Your Guest as a Cherished Friend:

Everyone likes to feel connected. Everyone likes to feel appreciated. Everyone wants to feel valued. When it comes to your approach to service, this is absolutely the case. Think about what you would do if you were having family or friends come in to stay for a week. You would likely make sure that they know how to find your house and that you were waiting to greet them when they arrived. If you didn't know their favorite drinks, foods, and television programs you would find out and then make sure to have those items on hand. You would find activities to do with them based on their likes and you would certainly be sure to clean up around the house before they arrived. Wouldn't you be sure that the beds were made and the bathrooms clean before they arrived? And while they were with you wouldn't you be sure that you made their visit fun and special by making them feel like the center of attention? I think most of us would go to these lengths to be sure that those who were important to us were well taken care of. When you think about the guests you and your team serve, these lessons are transferrable. Get to know your guests, understand what they need, what makes them happy, and how you can connect with them in small, but special ways.

Stay Positive and Friendly:

I am reminded of the bumper sticker "mean people suck" when I think about this philosophy. Every time I see it out there on someone's car, I think first, that bumper stickers seem like a lot of work. But after that, I think about how true that statement is in the marketplace. I often think about the energy folks waste being negative and how rubs off on those around them. Moods are as contagious as the flu in December, and anyone who has worked in a large business with lots of team members can attest to that. Have you ever been having an amazing day, a great day, a banner day, and then someone arrives at work with a dark cloud over their head and ruins the whole day for everyone? We've all been there and in this kind of instance it becomes abundantly clear that we are all divining rods for other people's moods and attitudes.

There are a few ways to keep a positive vibe alive with your guests and your coworkers. Remember that words matter, so how you say things has impact. Do you close at 5 or are you open until 5? Will you say no or find a way to say yes or compromise?

I was at a Starbucks a few weeks ago and when I ordered the dark roast of the day, the barista said "Great choice. We are brewing some hot fresh coffee right now and it will be ready in about 3 or 4 minutes. Are you okay with the wait or would you like Pike Place? I have that ready right now." She then offered to bring it out to me if I wanted to grab a seat while I waited. This was a nice alternative to "We are out of Komodo Dragon Blend - you'll have to wait."

Remember to keep in mind that every action will elicit a reaction in your guests and colleagues, so think through your words, tone of voice, and your body language. So much communication is nonverbal that you must be aware of the story you are telling without words. Don't let it paralyze you but keep it in mind as another way to use communication to build loyalty and trust.

Make it Easy:

Along the same vein of positivity is ease of use. When it comes to building loyalty, customer effort matters. Customers and consumers are always measuring how much trouble something is to accomplish with a business and that helps them determine to which organizations they will give their loyalty. It's a neat buzz word to talk about an effortless experience, which would be an ideal state, but better to look at making things as easy as possible to eliminate ambiguity and complexity.

Look at your core business from the point of view of the guest and then work to make sure that inconveniences are eliminated before they cost you business. You may hear about this in your Voice of the Customer (VOC) program or through interactions you have with them live in your business. The important thing is to look at the guest journey, end to end, throughout your business and make sure that everything lines up in a way that creates a seamless experience. Your customers may interact with you through a variety of channels and by taking the guest journey yourself you can smooth out the rough patches to ensure they don't become sources of aggravation. You may find in some instances customers are fine with self-service (assuming your content is well curated) and in other instances you may need live support. I think about the kiosks at the airport – these allow passengers to check in on their own and for the most part, they do a fair job. To supplement this and reduce overall choke points, the airlines have stationed attendants to check in on those who look to be having issues and there are always live agents at the counter for requests requiring a personal interaction.

It is up to you, your team, and your organization to make things as simple as possible for guests and eliminate points of potential hassle or inconvenience.

Thank Every Guest:

Gratitude is something we all crave – never more so than if you are an employee who has done something great or a guest who has given loyalty to a brand. When it comes down to it, there is no such thing as thanking a customer too much for his or her purchase or business. There are a lot of choices out there for most types of businesses, and the democratization of information via the internet makes everyone a much more informed consumer. Healthcare and higher education have learned much about this in the past decade as they fight for market share and solvency in this service and experience economy.

In the past, it was much more difficult to compare a college, hospital, doctor, or auto mechanic to the competition without a lot of legwork and time. Now, with just a few mouse clicks you can compare the patient surveys, yelp reviews, better business bureau reports, and best college rankings across the country. This again brings our story back to service when it comes to growing loyalty.

Think about the closing of a conversation with a guest – I refuse to think of them as transactions. When you or your team are in the final moments of speaking with a guest, this is time to finish on a high note. There is no better way to do that than with a sincere thank you and an invitation to return. I tend to fly American Airlines quite a bit and the counter personnel at the Detroit Metro Airport have come to recognize me when I check in. Although the kiosks are just fine, I tend to like to check-in with an agent to check upgrades and potential delays they might know about. They have taken to closing our conversations with "Have a great trip and we'll see you when you get back" or "Thanks for choosing American, Mr. Johnson. We'll see you next week." That's a nice touch in my opinion, especially in a space that is as maligned as cable companies and cell phone providers.

Remember, these canons are a great place to start with your service strategy. They can also help you create full guest engagement guidelines for your team. We will go into more detail on this in Chapter 19.

TAKE ACTION:

Think about the best way to engrain these standards into your team's daily actions. These key moves (and the service guidelines we will discuss later), are at the core of providing the kind of service that creates consistency and trust. From a place of trust and satisfaction, you can build loyalty and repeat business by reducing effort and anticipating guest needs.

- Are the principles of The Six Canons embedded into your daily work and training?

- How can you ensure that your internal customers (the team) feels the same care you want them to pass on to guests?

- Take the time to look at your company from the guest point of view. Visit your website, call your offices, walk into your business as a guest would. What are the hassles, inconveniences, and friction points that keep your guest's experience from being as easy as possible?

- Are you showing true gratitude to your team and are they showing gratitude to guests during every conversation?

TEAM
SUCCESS

4
. . . .

IT'S ABOUT SELECTION,
NOT HIRING

It's about right person, right fit, right time

UNLESS YOU ARE a company of one, you will need people to accomplish your goals and serve your guests or consumers. That means at some point you are going to have to choose people to join your organization and align them with your mission. To build a great team, a certain amount of discipline is needed when it comes to recruiting and selecting talent.

Let's start with recruitment. You can't select new team members if they don't apply or want to work for your organization. I have been through many talent droughts and if you don't have a competitive advantage that goes beyond pay, you will never have the talented and diverse work force you want and need to delight your guests.

I remember taking over a restaurant group in Ohio in 2011. We were having difficulties recruiting top notch

talent and it was taking a toll on our overall service. It
didn't take long to determine why we weren't getting
qualified applicants. There were issues with our engagement, our relationship with the union was not productive,
and our processes were not buttoned up in a way that
made for a good employee experience.

It took time to turn around our relationship with
our team and our reputation in the community – but the
work was worth it when we were able to recruit and retain
a top-notch work force. Satisfaction, sales, and efficiency
all saw vast improvement with better talent serving our
guests.

This leads me to the components of results-driven
selection. Let's walk through the key moves to building
strong teams through selection.

Cultivate a Great Reputation:

Remember, people in your industry and in your area talk.
Everyone around your business locations knows if your
business is a good place to work and they have no problem telling others. Your reputation goes a long way in
determining what caliber and quantity of applicants you
receive when positions come open. You can't hire folks
if they don't apply, and they will never apply if you aren't
a good place to work. Strike that, you will likely always
get applicants, but you won't have the depth of talent
from which to select if you don't have a strong reputation.
There will always be folks who will apply to work at locations that are bottom rung in terms of culture – but you
likely won't find them a match to the organization you are
trying to build.

Reputation can take on many forms. You may find that, like I did when I took on that Ohio account, that you have a culture that doesn't currently value people. Perhaps you have a reputation of being a financially driven, quality-is-nice-to-have type organization. Perhaps you've had complaints that have reached state agencies or bad press because of employee treatment. The good news is you can most always rehabilitate your image – if you have the time, energy, and wherewithal to do so. This isn't for everyone because it is a laborious process that can be soul sucking, but it worth it in the long run.

If you are taking over a turnaround and need to engage the workforce, there are a couple of surefire ways to do it (but they are painful). You have to dig for the truth and the root cause of the angst. This starts with listening – whether you call them town halls, listening tours, or engagement meetings they are crucial to improving your morale, culture, and reputation.

- Start by making it clear that honesty is needed, expected, and will be appreciated
- Ask the right questions
  - ◇ What is going well?
  - ◇ What isn't going well?
  - ◇ What are the main obstacles you are experiencing to doing your job?
  - ◇ What would you change to improve service?
  - ◇ If you could change anything – anything at all – about the company (regardless of cost, time, or resources) what would you do?

- Act quickly on the items you can correct with a short turnaround and follow up on items that might take longer or might not be possible. Often this is key because teams don't expect everything to be implemented, but they do expect follow up on every item they suggest.

- Report back on progress and let the team know what has been done and what is next – this is a great place to recognize those with ideas that have been implemented and seen positive results.

- Connect their suggestions to the action taken. This matters because you want to connect the dots from their ideas to what occurs because of them. Teams who are jaded or disengaged may not automatically make these connections and this is helpful to start building engagement.

These preceding five items are where I have started when it comes to rehabilitating business reputations for the better part of 20 years. When you think about the closed ecosystems that are present in most industries, it is no wonder that those seeking positions know the best (and worst) places to work.

Take Your Time:

Selection is not a contest that often rewards the quickest to pull the trigger. We've all been in crisis mode with hiring – especially if you are starting up a new business or opening a new branch. Either way you are starting from zero and that can be daunting, particularly if you have hundreds, or even thousands, of people to select for jobs. The best advice I ever received around selection had to do with being patient. I remember one of my early leaders telling me that you could select quickly, but if they don't work out and you have to start over, you'll end up taking more time in the long run. Think about having to recruit, interview, onboard, train, manage, and then ultimately replace that newly hired employee. There are also productivity downturns, on the job errors, and cultural erosion that can impact the organization when selection isn't a priority. If you want to quantify it, the Society of Human Resources Professionals (SHRM) says that the cost to replace an employee could be 6 to 9 month's salary. Others calculate as much a 1.5x – 2x a team member's annual salary to replace them. Between July, 2018 and February, 2019, from 2.3% to 2.4% of workers left their roles. That's between 3.4 and 3.5 million workers each month shuffling jobs. This is according to a combination of information from CNBC, Bloomberg, and the Job Openings and Labor Turnover Survey (JOLTS) from the Bureau of Labor Statistics (BLS). That is a tremendous expense and it isn't all job shopping (although with the low unemployment numbers, some of that undoubtedly was). Much of it was around misfits when it comes to roles, culture, or leadership. So, take your time and get a second opinion if needed to ensure you are bringing the right person for the right role into your family.

Watch the Candidate's Actions During the Interview:

Sometimes we get too locked into our interview guides and what we believe to be our innate ability to get the measure of people. When you interview, be sure to check your ego, that inflated sense of being a fantastic judge of people, at the door. If everyone was as good at sizing up people and talent as they purport to be, then we wouldn't have the massive job shifts we do each month. That said, one way to do this is to open up all your senses during the interview. When your candidate arrives attune to their actions.

Start with how they behaved when interacting with others:

- Were they nice to the receptionist or security person at the front desk? Remember they are going to be fairly nice to you since you are the one doing the hiring and hold the decision rights to select them or not. But do they value others who do not have that power?

- Did they hold the door open for someone as they entered or for you as you walked to the interview location?

- Did they greet people as you crossed paths with them in the hallway, elevator, or office?

- Are they smiling? Did they laugh? Do they seem genuine and friendly?

- Are they making friendly eye contact?

These are the kinds of behaviors you want your team members to exhibit on the phone or in person when they interact with people. And remember, even if you are selecting a person who may not directly serve guests, they will be serving those who do. Even those in finance, human resources, or marketing, who may not interact with guests, will still need these interpersonal and service skills to build your internal culture.

Hire the Attitude:

There are going to be a fair number of applicants who just aren't a fit for your organization. They either lack the attitude or aptitude – and this is where you may have a choice. Remember that in some cases you can absolutely train the skill if the candidate has an amazing personality. Of course, there are skilled trades that don't have any latitude, but do you really need a decade of experience running a cash register to make a great cashier? Absolutely not. Think carefully before you turn away a great smile and friendly nature (who knows, they may be right for a different position). If you are always recruiting and keeping your eyes open for talent, that will help you maintain a steady flow of applications that can lead to better hiring decisions. The other piece to this puzzle is patience. Sometimes you just have to wait when you haven't found the right candidate. Often your team may be begging for help and your managers may be complaining for you to hurry up already, but sometimes you just have to stick to your guns and wait for the right person. Most often, an empty spot is preferable to one with the wrong person occupying it.

Consider the Fit:

Is the person you are hiring a good "fit" for your organization. Now this may seem like cultural legerdemain but in actuality it should be at the very core of your selection process. As I mentioned above, having the right attitude is important, and that goes a long way toward ensuring a fit. But if the position calls for high energy, hiring someone with a more even keeled personality may not be a fit. You may have a job for that person at some point, but the job currently in question isn't it. You also have to consider the personalities at play in your current organizational dynamic. Simply put, you can't have a whole team of Type A Controllers or conversely, Passive Analyzers. Both are necessary but too much of a good thing leads to a leadership train wreck. If you lead a team, you have to consider your strengths and blind spots so that you can compensate them with the team you select. I can tell you that I struggle with process and organization, so I need help making sure the trains run on time. I select folks who understand the value of process and validation when it comes to sustaining success. Also, keep in mind if things like community involvement are a part of your cultural values then ensure that you are selecting with those traits in mind.

> *Hiring someone who doesn't fit with your organizational values will lead to frustration from you, the new team member, and their colleagues. They will never feel like a true part of the team and may even lead to the erosion of your culture if they become disengaged at work.*

Hiring someone who doesn't fit with your organizational values will lead to frustration from you, the new team member, and their colleagues. They will never feel like a true part of the team and may even lead to the erosion of your culture if they become disengaged at work.

Ask What-If Style Questions and Be Prepared:

If you have ever sat down for an interview with someone who is looking at your resume for the first time, you know how terrible an unprepared interviewer can be. I can say that I have been on both sides of that table and neither side wins in this situation. When you don't at least take a few moments to prepare yourself to meet a prospective candidate, it's a disservice to both. Remember that you are trying to make a good impression on the person you are interviewing just as much as they want to impress you. You may be trying to land some amazing talent to help improve your organization, so you have to be ready to wow the person you are interviewing as well. Remember that folks have choices as to where they work – and the more talented they are, the more choices they have.

Candidates are sizing you up as a leader because they don't want to end up working for a controlling, unprepared hack any more than you want an underqualified, apathetic team member. So, take a moment to be sure you come across as a leader worth following.

As for the questions, they matter, and you may well have an organizational interview guide that helps you navigate the process. Don't give this short-shrift, as we all tend to not love things that we are obligated to use. Remember that likely there are some solid questions in there, particularly if they give insight as to how a person thinks. You want to know what they would do in certain situations and how they would respond to roadblocks or problems. You want to hear that they have firm decision-making processes and that they use the breadth of their experience to find solutions. Now a cookie cutter interview guide isn't the whole answer – you have to look at the position and pose questions that have real meaning for that job.

- What would you do if a guest complained?
- How would you handle a guest who was belligerent?
- What does customer service mean to you?
- Tell me about a time when you went above and beyond for a guest.

These questions put your candidates in the driver's seat and allow them to really open up. Yes or no questions are great if you are a terrible listener and don't care what your future employee has to say - but we can all do better than that. Ask great questions, stop talking, and listen.

Let's dig in a bit more on interview guides. If you think your organizational version is lacking or needs updating, take the initiative to work with your Human Resources Department. I have worked with many HR professionals in my career and they are always very willing to help align for the types of candidates you are looking to recruit. Nothing gets solved if you grouse that "HR just doesn't get it." Rather help them craft a tool that will make your life easier when it comes to identifying the right talent.

Be Honest About Expectations and the Realities of the Job:

There are upsides and downsides with every job – be completely honest about them. Be up front about the hours for the job, the insurance benefits, pay rate, and opportunities for advancement. They will find out eventually anyway, so give them the chance to opt out of the interview before either of you wastes too much time. If you don't allow facial hair, if they will have to lift heavy things, or be required to work on holidays, let your applicants know. Also, be sure you give a realistic picture of what the job entails and what your expectations are for guest service. Make sure you emphasize the importance of caring for guests and that there is no wiggle room with that. When you discuss these types of non-negotiables during the selection process you will find that you are starting to reinforce your culture from the very beginning. If you do end up hiring the candidate, then she has already started her immersion into the values of the organization.

Also remember that it is important to reinforce that performance matters. It's great to be nice and willing to pitch in as part of a team and work holidays – but their overall execution will matter, too. Be sure that your perspective team members know that there are performance-based metrics, likely including service, productivity, and engagement scores, that will be monitored. You don't want them to think that they are completely managed via a scorecard or dashboard, but they need to know what success looks like and how they will be measured. It's also important that they understand that quality matters and a part of delivering great experiences is making sure that the products and services are spot on.

Treat Your Candidates Very Well:

Too often, interviewees aren't treated very well. Some old school leaders believe that as the hiring manager they have carte blanche to mistreat those who are seeking employment. First of all, that's a lousy attitude. It's hard enough out there when you are looking for a job without making it feel like a game show called "How Badly can I Mistreat You?" When you schedule someone in for an interview, be on time, offer them a bottle of water, and be prepared. Take the time to listen to what they have to say and come prepared with intelligent questions. Do them the courtesy of reviewing their resume prior to the interview to show you care. This will also help you craft questions specifically geared to learn more about the person as an individual. This is all by way of saying that the folks who are interviewing with you will walk away with more respect and loyalty to you and your business if you treat them well – and that applies whether or not they get the job. Which leads to the final point – be sure to let folks know in a timely manner if they weren't selected for the job so they can pursue other options. If you can give them feedback that might help them succeed next time, even better. Talk about building a world class reputation in the community!

Let Your Candidates Talk:

If you've ever been interviewed by a terrible listener, you know that sometimes it's more about the leader than their team. It doesn't do much good to ask a question to your candidate if you refuse to let them answer. When you interview, you are more of a moderator or game show host. It's about the person across the table, not you, so again, check that ego and be a great listener. Your goal in the interview is to get your candidate talking so you can learn about them and understand their strengths and weaknesses. I can tell you that the very best leaders I've worked for did a great job of always giving me enough oxygen in the room to make my point. This was obvious right away when I interviewed for my role or during our first meeting. They set the tone as a listener who wasn't afraid to share his or her point of view, but also wanted to hear mine. So, it's completely fine to let your personality and values shine through – in fact you should – but not at the expense of learning nothing about the person across the table.

Move Quickly:

This may seem counter intuitive based on one of the previous points, but once you've selected a candidate don't waste time getting them started. Let them give the requisite notice (but don't let them overdo it). I once had a candidate I really wanted to bring into the organization suggest four weeks' notice, which was sweet, but we decided that two would be just fine. You may even find that when they put in their notice, their current job releases them sooner – many organizations don't want folks coasting on the last two weeks or only being moderately present on the job. So, if they do get released early, be ready to bring them on sooner. Also note that once you extend a verbal offer, don't waste time getting their deal closed. Present them an offer letter quickly and then also move to complete all the steps needed to bring them onboard. Many folks won't even put in their notice at their current job until they have a formal offer, and those who are not currently employed may take another offer if they need to start working but you can't close the deal.

What Can They Teach You?

As a leader you want to be sure you are bringing team members into the organization that complement you and the rest of your team. Every time you select new talent you are adding to the knowledge, personality, and skill set of your organization. That can't be taken lightly. You can't have a team comprised all of folks who are exceptionally detail oriented or big thinkers; Not everyone can be a productivity focused leader. Everyone can't be obsessed with innovation. You can't have a whole group of folks who are thinking far into the future. You need a cross-section of those who are grounded in the now and those who are looking ahead.

Internal or External?

During the selection process be sure not to neglect your internal talent. Any chance you have to select from within will be a great way to engage your team – so long as they really are the best candidate. It has become taboo to talk about promoting from within without a fervent reverence, but I think you must balance that with the need for external talent as well. Never become so in love with your internal succession planning that you don't occasionally bolster your team from outside. It's easy for those who have come up through the ranks to fall in love with the organization and thus not be willing to challenge the current way of doing things. This can create a leadership group that refuses to change and believes that no one can do it better. The dangerous part here is the more successful and respected your organization is, the more you need the infusion of outside talent to keep you honest and competitive.

Remember as you bring new team members into your organization that there is a lot of pressure to get it right. It's not every day that you get the chance to infuse your organization with fresh energy. Every personnel change brings new ideas, enthusiasm, and diversity to your team. That is, it should. If you are considering selecting someone to join your organization and you aren't excited about what they are bringing, then take a beat to decide if they are a good fit for your team.

TAKE ACTION:

Remember that quality service begins with selecting the right team for the job. You cannot succeed without a great group of folks around you and that means picking the right individuals to create a winning team.

- What does your ideal team member look like? What are the key attributes that you need them to have for success?

- Where will you find great talent?

- How will you communicate the value of working for your organization?

- What is your reputation in the community, and do you need to improve it so you can attract the very best talent?

- Are you asking the right questions to identify those who have a spirit of service and quality engrained into their DNA?

- Are you bringing people into your organization that complement your existing team and add talents you currently lack?

- Are you balancing internal promotions and movement with outside talent?

5

. . . .

GETTING IT RIGHT WITH NEW TEAM MEMBERS

You selected them to join your family – now what?

WHEN I GOT my first job out of college, I was lucky to land at a small private university in Southern Indiana.

I was full of vim and vitality (and student loan debt) - and couldn't wait to get my career started. I had accepted a job outside of my degree for the potential to grow with a large organization, so I wasn't quite as well prepared for the job as I might have been. Along with the excitement of starting my new career was also the trepidation that comes with the unknown.

This could have gone a lot of ways, but I was fortunate that Mark was my new boss. The leader of the location where I started was one of "those" managers. He was respected and well known, and for good reason. He got results and he grew his people. I received a warm welcome on my first day, solid one-on-one time from Mark, and a detailed understanding of expectations. I also received a training plan that outlined my first two weeks which was used to drive my onboarding process. It was my constant companion as I learned the organization, and to this day I think it remains a great example of how to maximize the new team member experience.

> *When new team members start work, they are immediately judging their new organization and its culture – take advantage of this time to connect with them.*

When new team members start work, they are immediately judging their new organization and its culture – take advantage of this time to connect with them. There is a special honeymoon period when folks start new jobs and you can either choose to take advantage of this impactful time or let it go to waste. I challenge you to make the most of it.

What some fail to recognize is that onboarding is the first step of training and this begins to cement the relationship between organization and team member. When you take the time to ensure your new team members have a meaningful onboarding process several things happen:

- It acclimates them to the organization by making them feel comfortable
- They can meet colleagues and leaders so that they begin to feel connected
- They become familiar with expectations around

core items such as safety, service, ethics, and
work rules

- They see from the start that communication
  and care for the team is a priority
- They begin immersion into your culture to understand the mission, purpose, and benefits of
  working for your organization.

There are 5 ways you can make the most of your new
team member's onboarding process.

Welcome Them Warmly:

Remember that starting a new job is hard enough without
feeling unwelcomed. It is so important to show your new
team member around the business and introduce them
to everyone in their area. Also, make sure that your new
associate has all the basics that he or she needs to get
started. That could be the paperwork for direct deposit,
uniforms, name tags, or parking permits. This is a good
place to talk about name badges – first of all, please use
them. They are important to your brand and start every
interaction off by personalizing the Guest experience.
Second, resist the urge to slap a printed label on a cheap
blank and hand them out. This says, "I can pull that label
off and replace you anytime." That's not a great feeling
and is just one step above a "Hello My Name is" sticker
from the local convention. You can be better than just
price-of-entry here and have a welcome card signed by
the team or balloons on the new associate's desk. Anything that shows you are happy to have them on board is
a great way to start building loyalty and engagement.

Set the Expectation:

Folks can't hit a moving target or one that is kept a secret. If you did a great job during the hiring process, then you have already started sowing the seeds of expectation. There is no doubt that many service and execution misses aren't a lack of commitment, but rather a lack of understanding. Sometimes folks just don't know any better and that is a failure of leadership. Take the time during the first days to review the goals of the organization and what part the new employee has to play. Review their job description with them as well as how they should be spending their day. Most times when there is slack in a day and team members are not maximizing their time, chances are they haven't been set up for success. Make sure folks know exactly what they should be doing and that they have an organizational system to make it happen. Sometimes a $50 investment in software or planners can save you that much in lost time in just a week or less.

Train Them to Be Amazing:

Never forget that poorly trained associates give lousy service. That is just a fact – whether it aggravates team members or makes them feel undervalued, the impact is the same. When your guests come into your business, not only do they receive a substandard product or service, but they are met with an employee who hates what they are doing. This is sad, as it doesn't have to be that way. Too often, both managers and front line associates alike are tossed into roles with minimal or no training.

"Welcome. Here are the keys. Don't forget to lock up on the way out." – Sound familiar?

Many of us (myself included) have been trained this way. I have had supervisors who could barely toss me the keys and safe combination before they headed out the door. A stark contract to my first leader who took the time and put in the effort to make me successful.

Don't let your team start this way. When you hire a new team member, take the time to be sure they understand their jobs. This will often mean engaging new folks in all the learning styles – they need to be engaged by seeing, hearing, and doing. That is the only way that knowledge will be sure to stick. The best training happens when you can outline what the job looks like, script the critical moves of performance, then allow folks to try the skill in a safe place. If you are hiring someone to make a latte, best to have them practice a few rounds for the staff before you try to sell them to a guest. Remember that new associates should never be allowed to practice on guests, and they should have the opportunity to observe others doing the job to see what success looks like. Once they have a grounding in the basics, then they can have their big moment with guests under the supervision of a leader or key front-line associate. Leave nothing to chance and your guests will definitely approve.

Immerse Them in Your Culture:

If you want folks to buy in to your vision and values, you have to put them front and center from day one. Chances are your business, no matter how large, started small.

Take the time during onboarding to discuss your company's rich history and milestones. Many companies do a great job with starting by emotionally connecting new team members with their organization. Brands like Disney, Ritz-Carlton, and Southwest Airlines make this a focal point during onboarding. This is a big part of the reason why these brands have such great service and are associated with excellence. If it is important to you that you have spotlessly clean locations, say "my pleasure" instead of "thank you" or value quirkiness within your business, you must activate and model those behaviors. This is definitely not a place for do-as-I-say-and-not-as-I-do leadership. Honestly there is rarely a good time for that kind of leadership. Whether you have iconic videos, live presentations, PC based learning experiences, or hopefully a good mix of each, you have to make sure you tell your story and connect emotionally. Let new folks know just how important they are to the future of the business and ask them to give their best. Ask them to take great care of their guests. Ask them to help the team pull the rope in the same direction. You'd be surprised just how willing folks are to become a part of something bigger than themselves and embrace excellence.

Listen to Them:

When you are bringing new blood into your organization, don't waste a single moment. You have a fresh set of eyes and someone who has no vested interested in maintaining the status quo just because you've always done it that way. When folks begin with your organization talk to them about what ideas they have to make the organization stronger. Ask them what seems to be working well and what isn't - and how they would change things if they could. You should also make sure to ask them throughout the onboarding process how the experience has been for them and if things could have been done differently. Give them the freedom to speak openly and listen well. There is going to be gold in there because they have no filter or perspective on what has or has not been tried, or whose pet systems might be at work. They don't know anyone well enough to worry about offending them and there is a purity to the point of view of a new associate that can never be duplicated again. So, take notes and get ready to potentially have your processes challenged – then be prepared to champion these new ideas (if they ultimately make sense) and give away all the credit to your amazing new team member.

Remember the key here is to get your new team members started on the right foot and contributing quickly to the organization. But also, to ensure that they feel connected to the organization from the beginning and are immersed in your culture.

Ultimately the goal is to be sure that they are delivering stellar service to your guests and driving that deep loyalty that we all seek. That can't happen with a team that is hired and then left to their own devices. So, think through what great onboarding can be for your business and then engage your entire team to make it a reality.

TAKE ACTION:

New team members have taken a chance by joining your organization. When you bring someone onto your team, you are making a commitment to onboard and train them in a meaningful way. Onboarding represents a key opportunity to build trust and begin reinforcing your culture.

- What does your onboarding experience look like for new team members? If you haven't sat through the process and looked at it from a new employee's point of view, that should be on your list for the next onboarding cycle.

- Don't let team members begin work without making sure they understand the values of the company.

- Use onboarding to start immersing them in your culture and making sure they feel like part of the family.

- There should be a well scripted transition from selection to onboarding to training to working in live roles.

- Don't rely on excuses such as "I don't have time to train" or "there is no budget for that." When it comes to protecting consistent guest experiences and building trust, training and onboarding are the keys.

6

. . . .

UPPING YOUR TEAM'S GAME

Stop being afraid of managing performance

WHEN YOU START to notice that your team isn't performing at maximum potential, you have to move quickly. Performance management is a slippery proposition – and one that can very quickly deteriorate and erode your culture. This leads to spotty service, poor execution, and a potential exodus of your best team members.

As leaders, one of our key values must be to select, hire, train, and motivate the very best teams. That means that if performance is starting to slide that you have to do something about it. The attitude of ignoring it and hoping it gets better is not a winning strategy to be sure.

It begins with a kind hand. Remember that unless we are talking about insubordination or a violation of business rules, then chances are we are talking about modifying daily behaviors. There is a good chance that if you bring the hammer for small infractions, you'll lose the person altogether. While speed and quick action is necessary, you can absolutely do so in a way that doesn't send your associate into a further downward spiral.

Let's talk about what to do when you notice that your team may not be firing on all cylinders:

Make Sure They are Crystal Clear About Expectations:

Often front-line associates lament that they didn't know what the expectations were from their leaders, thus making it hard to hit the target. Sometimes this is just a ploy to deflect, but often it is an accurate assessment. During the selection process, through training, and into daily work, you should make it abundantly clear what the expectation is for work performance. If there is an expectation of working less than glamorous hours, the need to be nice to guests, dress policy, or required production targets, these should not be surprises to your team. Make sure they understand the need for fantastic safety as well as the base pieces of their job. Training can absolutely help here, as those who are well trained in their jobs report better overall satisfaction and engagement – which leads most times to delivering a quality experience to guests. When it comes to training, this is not the place to skimp and also not a place to make excuses about your lack of training budget or time. Be creative with micro training, cross training, and virtual-training to ensure your team has the skills they need.

Ensure They Understand Where They are Falling Short:

Your team can't improve if they don't understand where things are going off the rails. Chances are we are not talking about huge miscues, but rather small misses. The problem with small executional issues is that they snowball quickly and before you know it, your organization can be in crisis mode. Worse than that, once the attitude of "no one knows what is going on around here" starts to permeate your atmosphere, it can poison even your best team members. If performance issues aren't dealt with, one of two things will happen. Those with the best work ethic and execution will begin to execute at a lower level on par with their colleagues or they will just leave your organization for a better opportunity. Dealing with performance issues is tough stuff – let's face it, anytime you have to sit someone down and tell them they aren't cutting it is a tough day. And it's okay that you feel that way, because it keeps you grounded in the idea of being kind to folks, even when the conversation is around their need to improve. You must be straightforward and right to the point, but you don't have to be rude or unfeeling. Remember that the hope is that their work will improve, and they will remain a part of your organization, but for that to happen you can't mince words. Let them know precisely what is not meeting the standard and what success looks like. Also, be sure they understand the impact on the business, the guests, and the team when they don't perform at a high level.

Craft a Path Back to Success Together:

When you finish the conversation around performance, it isn't enough to just tell your team members where they are falling short and then leave them to figure it out on their own. Most associates in that position will absolutely fail. There are those that find motivation in adversity and will pull themselves out on their own, but a majority will likely crumble and be gone from your organization soon. There was a reason why you hired your team members, so helping them course correct their performance will bring the value to the team that you must have seen in them at one time.

> *Make it clear that they are responsible ultimately for upping their game, but that you are there to help them along the way.*

Make it clear that they are responsible ultimately for upping their game, but that you are there to help them along the way. Make sure you give them your opinions and ideas, and craft an action plan together to bring things back in line. Performance plans or action plans have a bad name out there in the business universe – but only because leaders don't use them right. Take the time to craft a plan that shores up training deficiencies and highlights behavioral changes that will lead to results. Involve the associate in the creation of the plan and then meet regularly to review. You must invest in the process as well if it is to succeed.

So, remember, performance management can be uncomfortable. But like everything else it gets easier over time.

Remember, You Can't Save Them All:

You are going to believe as a leader that you can save everyone - that if you lead well enough, train hard enough, push often enough that you can pull everyone up with you. Chances are that's not going to be the case and poor service will result when you don't take that final step of removing folks from the organization. Most of us wait too long to take this step, either because we think we can save them, or we feel handcuffed by the rules of our organization. Those are convenient excuses because discipline and termination are hard.

It shouldn't be the knee jerk response to every issue, but you can't continue to coach team members for the same things over and over again and see no results. You must build your case, document your findings, coach with vigor, and encourage with heart – and then take action if nothing happens. Once you have your information collected, it's easy to make your case to HR and follow the process. I haven't met an HR professional yet who didn't endorse separation if the evidence was there that performance was lacking. When they do push back is when you don't have your information complete or haven't trained someone properly. In those cases, the failure is on the leader, not the team member.

Remember, the earlier you catch performance issues, the easier they are to correct. When you wait too long, you'll have a real uphill climb on your hands. It also begs repeating that when you select talented team members, train them well, and treat them with respect, they are less likely to have performance issues or leave your organization.

TAKE ACTION:

How is the performance in your organization? Does your team know the expectations and are they delivering upon their performance goals?

It's important that teams understand not only that they are responsible for owning service in their particular areas, but also for supporting each other through teamwork to drive the guest experience.

- Are you providing candid feedback to your team about expectations and performance?

- How do you handle those who are not meeting standards and expectations?

- Take the time to implement performance plans and goals to move team members back on the right path.

- Follow up regularly when it comes to owning performance plans – it is the responsibility of the team member, but they shouldn't be in it alone. Give feedback and encouragement to help them succeed.

- While painful, sometimes you will need to move those who cannot get on track out of the organization. Waiting too long can create a toxic work environment.

7
. . . .

THE REWARD
RECOGNITION SYSTEM

Recognition comes from the heart,
but sustaining it takes discipline

PEOPLE LOVE TO know when they've done a great job.

It energizes them. It gives them purpose. It reinforces the positive behaviors.

And it makes them hungry for more.

When I was first beginning in leadership, I had my team approach me to say that they thought I was too negative. They told me that I was always telling them what they did wrong and never seemed to see what they did right. That hurt, because in my head I thought I was doing an amazing job of recognizing their good works and rewarding them when they got it right.

So, I took a hard look at my behavior and realized that I wasn't doing as great a job as I thought I was.

I logged my interactions with my team, and it really did show me where I had work to do with my gratitude.

You can try it yourself.

Keep a journal every day for one week documenting each interaction with your team and what you discuss. Be detailed, note positive versus negative comments, and evaluate the ratio. This isn't anything difficult, but sadly most folks will never take the time to look at their behavior with the same level of scrutiny with which they evaluate their teams. Take the time to do this today (you can easily capture on your smart phone or tablet) and then see if you are hitting a good ratio.

When I tallied up my results, I was very disappointed in my efforts because what my team told me was true. I was terrible at recognition, but I made the decision then and there to make gratitude a priority.

Am I perfect? Not even close. To this day, I must work to make recognition a priority in my every day leadership.

So why is it so critical to be great at recognition? Because it drives the behaviors you seek and motivates your team to provide amazing customer service.

Happy team members who feel like they are valued by their organizations, deliver much better Guest service. It is driven by the reflective nature of your team and the feel-good impact of positivity.

Happy team members who feel like they are valued by their organizations, deliver much better Guest service. It is driven by the reflective nature of your team and the feel-good impact of positivity.

So, to illustrate the importance of recognizing amazing behaviors, here is a system that will help keep it top of mind.

If you want to win with employee engagement, follow the R.E.W.A.R.D. Recognition System.

Recognize Great Behaviors.

Everyone Deserves Recognition.

Winning Is Cause for Celebration

Accentuate the Positive

Rewards Come in All Sizes

Deputize Everyone to Help

Let's break it down and talk about it in detail:

Recognize Great Behaviors:

Start by taking the time to reward and celebrate the wins. There is no doubt that amazing things are happening in your business every single day, but you have to stop long enough to see them. There is wisdom in taking time to stop and just observe what is happening in your organization every day. The other tip here is to be timely. There is nothing less impactful than waiting too long to give out kudos for a job well done. Remember there is a half-life to appreciation and the clock is ticking, so don't wait for the perfect moment – just jump in there and recognize! The other piece of recognition is to understand that specificity matters. Don't waste breathe on compliments like "thanks for all you are doing." That is meaningless blather with absolutely no impact. Find something specific to praise when it comes to recognition and that will increase the impact exponentially.

Everyone Deserves Recognition:

Recognition cannot be hoarded or used for only certain portions of the work force. There is a philosophy out there that purports that only front line associates or front line managers are worthy of praise and recognition. That seems like a giant pile of nonsense wrapped in a rainbow of shenanigans. If someone does a great job, tell them. While these team members are vital to the guest experience, there is no level of an organization where magically folks don't need to know they are important or that they matter to the company. Take a moment to ask yourself if there are gaps in your recognition plan and then attack that void. Chances are you'll start impacting an underappreciated segment of your organization and they'll appreciate it greatly. In my conversations with middle managers – district managers, area managers, regional managers – they report a constant state of underappreciation. That is dangerous because this level of most companies is responsible for translating organizational thought into field action. If this swath of leadership loses motivation or departs the organization, it can leave a void when it comes to culture and accountability.

Winning Is Cause for Celebration:

Nothing should be rewarded more emphatically than behaviors that further your guest's needs or organizational
agenda. It is even more important if you are in the middle of a change effort – feel free to go overboard on items
that are in lock step with your values and mission. Too
often, during times of change, there is so much attention
to keeping the organization between the guard rails that
appreciation is neglected. When you are lucky enough
to have advocates who are really championing your goals
and values, you will accelerate your success if you call out
those who are helping you win. Trust me, it will help the
rest of your team fall in line. Once the team sees what
you as a leader value and what the business rewards, they
will look to repeat those items as they seek additional
recognition.

Accentuate the Positive:

There is nothing that kills an organization like negativity.
There are staggering statistics out there that show that
75% of those who leave organizations are quitting their
bosses, not their jobs. That is just one stat from Gallup,
but other data suggests it could be as high as 80%. One
of the biggest reasons that folks make a change is because
their direct supervisors don't take the time to give them
a pat on the back. Ensuring your teams feel valued and
appreciated isn't that difficult. You can recognize a great
safety behavior, a positive guest interaction, or a clean
work space. If you take the time to really watch folks
during their work day, you'll definitely find things worth

calling out. Don't wait for the big moment, but rather reward accomplishments of value – if you wait for the bulletin board moments, you'll miss the bits of everyday magic. A good rule of thumb is a 3:1 ratio of positive to negative ratio feedback to your team. Why? Because if you call out the great stuff your team is doing, they will be far more likely to correct negative actions when you bring them to their attention. Plus, if you take the time to give good feedback, they won't assume every time you walk toward them they are about to get scolded. But don't fall into the compliment sandwich conundrum as that is a surefire way to confuse your team. When I hear leaders layer in performance management between praise, it is very frustrating. Rather than anyone appreciating the gratitude or taking the feedback to heart, it leaves people scratching their heads in confusion and not learning anything.

Rewards Come in All Sizes:

It is no secret that rewards are necessary and appreciated by teams at all levels of the organization. Those rewards can take many shapes and should be crafted to fit the achievement. Sometimes a pizza party for the team will be appropriate. Other times you may give out movie tickets. And still other times a hand written thank you note will do the trick. Often it is enough to stop and say thank you face to face. The key is to scale the reward to accomplishment and understand how your teams like to be recognized. Remember that some folks are very private and would like their appreciation quickly behind closed doors and others like their "moment" to be more public.

The key is to know your team well enough to make those distinctions and then act accordingly.

Deputize Everyone to Help:

No one is exempt from providing recognition. Anyone who can't be bothered to show the love to their team or think they are above such things must be inspired to change. Encourage and motivate your teams to want to provide amazing recognition by working hard to be great at it yourself. If you show everyone how important it is to you, and make sure the entire team sees you in action, you will motivate your teams to make it a priority as well. Also, make sure you give everyone the power recognize. That could mean a program such as thank you cards for a monthly drawing that anyone can give to anyone. Think about giving all team members a certain amount of thank you cards they can use each month. Encourage them to use these to recognize colleagues and then have them placed in a pool for a prize drawing. Find out what your team values and then make that the prize. Your team may value grocery store gift cards, vacation days, or movie tickets – make sure the value and type of gift is appropriate to your organization. Remember that these do not have to be gigantic awards; even the smallest rewards can have impact when coupled with sincere gratitude.

This kind of peer to peer recognition we are discussing is the purest and most powerful recognition there is and it means a great deal to team members. Wait until you observe a front line associate give a card to their boss or a cashier write a card to a custodian. It is powerful and awe inspiring – and the best part is that it drives a culture of appreciation that cannot be rivaled.

Some organizations try to drive accountability around recognition by setting up recognition goals for leaders. Quotas tend to take the blood out of recognition and make it seem like another box to check, but you have to keep track of those who may be having trouble in this area. It's a line we all have to walk – between pure, inspired appreciation and the need to track the amount of recognition being given organizationally.

So, take some time to head out and catch your team doing something (or hopefully lots of things) right. You will be inspired by the amount of daily magic your teams are creating.

TAKE ACTION:

Think about recognition as reinforcement for the behaviors you seek. When your team sees what you and the organization value through recognition, they are more likely to repeat those key moves. This improves the team experience, increases engagement, and leads to a more predictable guest experience.

- Don't wait for the huge moments to recognize. Show value in the everyday excellence that leads to consistent magic and delight.

- Inspire team members to recognize each other – peer to peer recognition has power and can improve teamwork.

- It becomes easy to recognize the same folks repeatedly for doing the same great job. Keep encouraging them but also look for the best in others to help them develop and flourish.

8

....

STOP KILLING CREATIVITY

Your team is a powerful catalyst for innovation

MOVIES AND TV shows such as Lucy, Limitless, and Pinky and the Brain weave in the popular legend that says we only use a small percentage of our brain. The myth goes that if we could just bust loose that remaining 90% we would be unstoppable geniuses that could freeze time, write novels in a day, and control the universe.

Now these are all nonsense to be sure, and magazines such as *Scientific American* have debunked this as a plot premise.

But that doesn't mean that we can't use our brains more effectively to improve the guest experience. On any given day we are presented with problems and hiccups that must be dealt with and issues that need to be resolved. While process is indeed the great equalizer and allows for consistent service, there are often challenges that require a creative approach to solve. Our capacity to dream, create, and inspire change is something we cannot neglect, as it will pay dividends when we need it most.

Creativity and innovation are the life blood of the Guest experience. Period!

Today's marketplace begs us to be creative – it looks us in the eye and dares us to delight and amaze. It urges us to push for more and demands to be surprised. Now in the interest of full disclosure, today's guests want it all. They want a consistent experience that takes care of the all the basics in a way that feels trustworthy and authentic. On the other hand, they want to be surprised by occasional wows and new ideas so that they don't get bored.

Customers have access to all of your competitors via technology, and that flow of information in the palm of their hands leads to them benchmarking you against many different businesses. The internet ensures the democratization of information in a way different from previous generations. This means that they not only are comparing you to your direct competitors but to anyone they can research. So, you must look beyond your particular industry for great ideas and market disrupters. Everyone is your competition.

When I see businesses from my youth such as Toys 'R' Us and Blockbuster gone from our retail spaces and I watch the struggles of other such as Sears and J.C. Penney, I wonder how innovation could have kept them more relevant. Think about it, Sears practically invented the mail order catalogue business. They were the place to go if you wanted tools and hardware. As I write this book, they are in bankruptcy court and it is unclear if they will survive.

It's easy to call out ideas after the fact, from the cheap seats, but as I loved all these brands I wonder:

- Would Blockbuster have survived if they had purchased Netflix and embraced mail order and streaming?

- How could Toys 'R Us have fared if they would have embraced technology and changing generational buying habits? They likely were hurt by guests who "show roomed" (using physical store fronts to research a product before buying it online for a discount).

- Is J.C. Penney's model still sustainable in this era of enormous big box versus small boutique – are they caught in an unsustainable middle ground?

So how to do you drive that amazing innovation in your business? How do you inspire the team to bring you their very best? How do you nurture and fan the flames of smoldering thoughts to ignite into the passion that drives fantastic service?

I think Best Buy is a story to watch. They were in the same spot as other retailers as Amazon was gaining share and folks like me were looking at cameras and laptops in the store before ordering them at a discounted price online. They started price matching the products and even offered space to brands like Samsung and Apple to showroom their products in their stores. Finally, the addition of services such as The Geek Squad gave guests a reason to visit the store.

As you seek to inspire your teams to innovate and dream, keep the following in mind:

Don't Be Scared to Make Mistakes:

Understand that mistakes are a biproduct of risk taking. There is no doubt that you have to minimize the damage, but if you make your team fearful of miscues then you'll find they will deliver "vanilla" work. Vanilla is safe and easy. Vanilla doesn't pose risk. But vanilla will only delight your customers for so long. You need to get your team to dig deep and try new things. I once had a boss pull me in and tell me that he was tired of seeing me play it so safe.

"Stop pulling the trigger ten times and getting it right ten times," he said. "Start taking 100 chances a day and get 90 right! That's more fun for everyone."

He was right. It was more fun.

Encourage your team to share new ideas and reward those who do so, regardless of whether the idea is a success. Remember, the idea isn't to find all winners, but to get the juices flowing. Chances are even the bad ideas will inspire good ones to come along.

Inspire your teams to take chances and experiment – just be sure to never experiment on customers.

Inspire your teams to take chances and experiment – just be sure to never experiment on customers.

Create a Safe Place to Nurture Ideas:

Your team is hungry to be able to share their ideas and will appreciate the chance to give them voice. Make your peace with the fact that not all ideas will be amazing. In fact, like we mentioned above, they may start off down-right terrible. The magic happens when everyone feels respected and valued enough to give their honest opinions. There are going to be bad ideas and that's okay – just don't pretend that they don't exist. Sometimes you have to be honest with your team and colleagues to make sure that all ideas are valued but honestly evaluated. It should also be true that when ideas are critiqued that everyone should be treated with dignity and respect so that the team doesn't get discouraged.

Be careful not to confuse respect with placation, because if honesty isn't present in idea meetings, you'll find that no one can grow. It might sting for a moment, but in the long run, it will help folks to grow, evolve, and mature. The output will be better ideas more quickly.

Promote Robust Communication:

When there are lots of rules and everyone is uptight about who talks to who, the creative process just dies. When someone can pick up the phone and excitedly talk to someone about their big ideas without worrying about the org chart, then you are well on your way to success. When I abandoned protocol about sharing ideas throughout my career, I have found my creativity reached new heights. I also found when I became less uptight about title and ceremony, my team had much better, more off the wall, game changing ideas. You will find that rules do nothing but bind up a team's creativity and keep their innovative thoughts from shining through. Allow folks to be open with ideas and share them with everyone.

Improvement is Innovative, Too:

Often organizations get so focused around what's new, they forget to look at what needs to be improved. Consider that continuous improvement is also a key piece of innovation because it improves the overall experience and contributes to the flavor of innovation. You could also see a current product or offering in your marketplace that has the potential to be taken to a new level. Think of how Amazon has changed how we shop, how Netflix and Vudu have changed how we watch movies at home, and how mobile ordering has changed how we enjoy coffee forever. So, as you walk your organization and consider your execution, think about if there is a better way to drive the guest experience. Can service be better, faster, cheaper, or more personalized? Even the smallest changes can drive big improvement. The trick is to also engage your teams in the conversation to get their thoughts on improvement and don't shy away from change just because you have always done things a certain way.

Pilot in a Safe Place:

As you continue to try new things, it's important to test them in a safe place. Depending on the size of the change, you should work to mitigate the potential risk to guest experience and organizational efficiency. Remember also that when you limit risk, you also make it easier to be forgiving of mistakes as mentioned earlier. Find a core piece of your business that is representative and then take your best shot with the new service or product. This is a great way to be fast to market, make mistakes, learn from them, and then be ready with the next iteration of the process or product. Listen to customer and team feedback and move quickly to change based on the feedback received. This not only helps your business work in a more innovative fashion, but also speeds up feedback and the ability for colleagues to help move an idea forward by adding their commentary.

There is no silver bullet to creativity except to not get hung up on being right all the time. Make sure that you embrace mistakes, use them to get better, and don't give up. Make sure that your mistakes don't impact the guest experience and that those who are brave enough to share ideas are respected for doing so.

No one likes to be critiqued, that's a given – but if we all just leave our egos at the door and make the effort to provide constructive versus destructive feedback, you will find that your organization can absolutely find its innovative flare.

Customers are positively delighted when you deliver on your brand promise every single day and never allow your service to become stale or stagnant.

TAKE ACTION:

Your customers have a line of sight into innovation that is sometimes about being first to market, but could also be about improving upon a model that is already successful. Think of how Netflix has improved upon the home movie watching experience. Inspire your team to share ideas, take chances, and learn from experimentation.

- Who are your customers comparing you to? Think outside your industry as well as within.

- Are you encouraging idea sharing from your team?

- Be sure to look at new ideas at the same time you are looking to improve your current products and services.

- Don't criminalize mistakes. Learn from them and use them as opportunities to improve.

LEADERSHIP SUCCESS

9
· · · · · · · · · · · · · · ·

COMMUNICATING
WITH PURPOSE

*It is your responsibility
to be sure you are understood*

AS I AM in the process of writing this book, George H. W. Bush, our 41st president of the United States has just died. I heard on the news just last night that he is no longer with us and there have been many articles in the newspaper and on television outlining his life and accomplishments.

Now I'm in no way veering off into politics in this book. I learned a long time ago that the quickest way to clear the dinner table was to bring up religion or politics. Not that having opinions and such isn't great – and everyone is absolutely entitled to theirs – but if you want to keep things friendly, these topics are generally land mines.

But back to President Bush. I believe that many of our presidents have something to teach us about leadership and building consensus. There is no doubt that we all could do a better job in our leadership and inclusivity (presidents included), but that doesn't mean we can't learn from one another. This matters because if you are in the middle of leading a change effort around guest experience, team engagement, or creating culture you will need to communicate a clear and compelling vision. You will need to build coalitions as you win hearts and minds. If you can communicate your vision for culture and service in a way that compels action and enthusiasm, you will find that your mission will be significantly easier.

Without communication, you can't build relationships or deliver great service.

All of this said, I had no idea that President Bush was such a prolific letter writer. It seems he penned thousands in his lifetime, and they were all written with purpose and enthusiasm. He never put pen to paper without purpose and he understood the power of communication to not only move public opinion, but to foster relationships.

This hit me as I watched folks extol the virtues of this past president. It wasn't about his presidential legacy as much as it was about fostering relationships and keeping in mind that, in the end, connections are what matter most.

So, when you communicate with team members, colleagues, friends, or family, think about how you can make the most of every word. There is power in words and the attention you take when you select your language and medium make a difference.

1. **Pick Your Medium Carefully:**
   Its easy to fall back on the communication method with which we feel most comfortable. These days many favor text messages and emails, and those may be fine based on the kind of communication you are trying to send. Would thank you wishes for a job well done be best sent with emojis in a text message, would they be received better as an email with full sentences and a copy to colleagues, or would the well wishes be most resonant as a card or letter written by hand and mailed to the high achiever's home? The answer is yes.

   This is situational to be sure and very much based on the person to whom you are sending the note. It is possible that for a small item that was well done that a text message, high five, or a few quick words may brighten someone's day. You could always go with the idea of the larger the accomplishment the grander the recognition. That's a fair way to approach it. It's also reasonable to assume that generationally there could be considerations here as well, so keep that in mind. For example, I don't have much use personally for text message recognitions. I see their value and I have colleagues who think they are great, but for me I'd rather have an email that took a moment to craft and seems a little more formal. Of course, if you have a recognition system that allows you to send out quick notes via technology that could potentially resonate as well.

And honestly, you never can go wrong with a hand-written note. There is something special about putting pen to paper, so if you want to make an impression and likely give someone a recognition that will be kept and appreciated, pull out your best pen and go to work. Even now as I look around my office, I have thank-you notes on my wall that I framed from over the years. They are a combination of hand written and typed, but they are all hand signed and were delivered through the mail. Each one, whether from a former boss or a group to whom I spoke, has special significance to me and they will likely stay on my wall for some time to come.

2. **Don't Just Communicate with Those You Agree with:**

It's easy to take the time to communicate with those we agree with or like, but often not as easy with those we have friction with. That's human nature. We like things that are comfortable and what's more comfortable than interacting with those who are of a similar mind. That doesn't mean it's the most productive use of our time, though. George H. W. Bush took the time to craft letters to many, and likely the hardest had to be the letter he wrote to Bill Clinton after losing the 1992 presidential election. My favorite line from that letter was "I am rooting hard for you." The fact that he took the time to start repairing their relationship after that hard-fought

campaign teed up a long future of working together for global relief efforts after natural disas-
ters, tsunamis, and floods.

Be sure you take the time to reach across your
particular aisle. Take the time to communicate
with coworkers, direct reports, and team members with whom you don't agree. That friction
may be just what you need to ignite a great idea
or solve a problem. Great achievements are
rarely made by rooms full of people who think
the same way. So, stay engaged with everyone,
because that kind of constituency sets you up for
success when leading a cultural change effort.

Changing hearts and minds is a tough business
and you'll need all the support you can get.
When you stay connected to both those who
agree with you and those who don't, you are
uniquely positioned to connect all the departments and work groups in your organization.
You'll need everyone coming together to place
guests at the center of your operational thinking,
so never miss a chance to communicate your
thoughts and vision. This also sets you up to
receive feedback from various points of view and
backgrounds, which will strengthen your thinking and thicken your skin. You'll need both as
you push, pull, drag, and cajole your organization to a new state where customers are always a
consideration in the decision-making process.

3. **Communicate with Purpose:**

   Think back to the most worthless email you received from someone in your organization yesterday. It likely suffered from one of a few fatal communication flaws. This probably made it tough to decipher what you were supposed to do with it and you likely deleted it waiting on additional clarity.

   That is something you should consider each time you push send on an email. When you begin to communicate your vision and ask for resources, you must dial in your messaging. This means taking the time to determine what you want out of a communication and that your call to action is clear. There is a great anecdote about Steve Jobs that he only put 1 request per email to eliminate confusion about what he was requesting or sharing. That's a good rule of thumb – at least keep the focus on a single theme in each communication, note, or email.

It is easy in any communication to run on and on with exposition and explanation but adhere to the 1:2:3 rule. Keep to one topic, request no more than two actionable items, and give no more than three examples, metrics, or supporting information bullets to show why what you are sharing matters.

It is easy in any communication to run on and on with exposition and explanation but adhere to the 1:2:3 rule. Keep to one topic, request no more than two actionable items, and give no more than three examples, metrics, or supporting information bullets to show why what you are sharing matters. You may think that only three supporting items sounds thin but remember that most folks aren't going to read past the first three anyway (or if they do, they won't remember them). Also, if you provide more than three you haven't taken the time to summarize and combine where appropriate and the others are likely pretty thin. If you feel you must share more than three, then formulate the information into a three bulleted executive summary type communication and attach the remaining data as a sort of appendix. If more information is requested, be sure you are clear about the timing for the turnaround and then beat that time by 24 hours whenever possible.

Keep your topic laser focused on the one topic you are discussing. If it is about employee engagement, stick to it. If it is about field training and deployment, stay tuned in to that. Share the what, how, and when, then move to what you need. If it is information only, then be clear that no action is needed other than review and feedback. If you need an action taken or funding, then be sure you set a date when you need the resources in place and follow up prior to your drop-dead date.

4. **Be Positive:**

    You can't let yourself be the person that is always grousing, complaining, or rocking the boat. Now you should be the person who regularly pushes things past the point of comfort for the good of the customer, but you have to walk a fine line.

    You must measure your approach so that you are reinforcing your messaging with positive stories of guest satisfaction and employee engagement, and how various departments and disciplines can support each other to improve the guest experience. There is a subtle art to disruption. It is easy to look at the classic disrupters such as Jeff Bezos and Steve Jobs and be inspired to metaphorically slap everyone in the face in your organization. Take it from someone who has spent decades in corporate America – that is a quick way to become labeled as a dissident and slowly (or not so slowly) be worked out of the organization.

    But if you stay positive in the face of naysayers and find connections that grow into positive interactions, you'll find that you can slowly layer in values you wish to imbue into your business. It isn't an overnight proposition, and often it is painfully slow, but you can harness the power of positive language to move your organization to a more customer-focused mindset. Share credit when appropriate, stroke the egos that need stroking, and make sure that you mix in positive commentary with the burning need to change before you lose market share.

5. **Show Gratitude:**

As you work to move your organization to a more guest-centric way of thinking, you will find many who are on board with your thinking. You will find coaches, informal mentors, and early adopters who are hungry to act on what you are creating.

Keep in mind that if you don't show appropriate gratitude and recognize those who are contributing to the customer focus, you may find they become apathetic or disengaged. Take time to thank those who are helping you move the needle and make sure that their managers know how much help they have been. Likely that will lead to additional recognition and visibility – and once something is proven to be successful, everyone wants to be first on the list to get it.

As you work on your customer service tools and training, you'll need to get opinions, those to pilot the training, and statistics that show what you are creating has value. The more you show gratitude to those who help you along the way, the more likely they are to continue and the more likely you are to gain supporters along the way.

Most employee engagement surveys discuss communication as something that needs to be improved. This is a catch all metric that covers everything from "I am unclear about our larger purpose" to "no one knows what is going on around here."

Fostering great communication is one of the most important things a leader can do – it is a foundational element of driving culture and inclusion. Every day you have the power to ensure that everyone is heading in the same direction and to keep everyone well informed about what matters most.

Pre-shift huddles are a key tool for this. Whether you call them huddles, line ups, meetings, or rallies, these short but impactful meetings are welcome in all disciplines. It doesn't matter whether you work in retail, healthcare, manufacturing, or theme parks, you can benefit from this daily practice. In these short meetings you can communicate with your team, deliver micro training, and recognize great work; these are the key points that most front-line teams want their leaders to improve upon.

I have seen these meetings delivered and work very well in an array of different businesses throughout my travels. I have seen pre-shift meetings with TSA agents prior to shift change in airports. I observed them for years when I worked in restaurants and retail. I have even observed associates at the Apple Store meeting just prior to opening their doors. They all had a couple of things in common: they were interactive, fun, high energy, and full of relevant information.

Remember that planning for these meetings is one

of the most important pieces to success and impact. Pre-planning and preparation will help you make the most of your time with your team. Gather them at the same time and same place each day and cover a few key topics.

1. Daily Focus: What matters most today? Is there a sales goal, safety goal, service goal, or customer need that is top of mind?

2. Wins and Losses: Be sure to cover what is going well and where you need to improve. Engage the team in creating solutions.

3. Voice of the Customer (VOC): What are your Guests saying? Call out the good and the bad, and use this as a time to look for ways to improve or recognize those performing well. Be honest about where you are with your scores versus where you want to be.

4. Notices: While not the place to get mired in rules, this is a good place to share new polices or changes to work rules that are important for everyone to know.

5. Recognition: Take time to celebrate goals and shout out those doing great work. Encourage the team to recognize each other as well.

Keep in mind that these meetings are short, but their impact will be felt all day long. They are easy to neglect and to skip when you are short staffed, busy, or under stress. Don't let them get pushed off of your schedule by other priorities. If you are struggling to implement staff huddles, then start small. Gather the team together for just a minute and talk about safety. Then once that is comfortable, add another minute on service. Slowly grow the meeting until you are at that 10 to 15-minute time-frame and then don't let it go much longer. Sometimes just getting started is the hardest part, so make the commitment and gather the team for as long as you can to get the meetings off the ground.

Always remember that communication is a bed-rock element of team engagement and if you keep it open, clear, and authentic you'll find that your team will be more open to giving additional discretionary effort. Most team members will do the basics, but only a certain amount will do the right thing when no one is looking. That extra little bit you need from your team to differen-tiate yourself in the marketplace lies in that discretionary effort – the things team members choose to do when they don't necessarily have to do so.

Team members are more likely to exercise this good judgment when they feel secure and well informed, and robust communication can build that environment.

TAKE ACTION:

Great communication leads to employees who feel as though they are well informed, well trained, and given an environment in which they can thrive.

When it comes to communicating, be sure to:

1. Choose the right medium or channel
2. Communicate with everyone, not just those who agree with you
3. Communicate with purpose
4. Be positive in your communication
5. Show gratitude for those who help you and your mission

- How will you communicate with your team?

- What team members or colleagues are you not engaging – and how will you open a dialogue with them?

- Do you have a focused communication strategy or are your messages long winded train wrecks?

- Are you taking a positive tone with your messaging and showing gratitude – while being honest about what is needed to drive a service culture?

10

· · · · · · · · · · · · · · ·

CHANGE IS NOT FUELED BY SPREADSHEETS

People drive change, not action plans.

IF YOU ARE going to build a service culture, it will likely involve some element of change. If you were satisfied with the current state of your service – or if you didn't see benefit to upping your game – you wouldn't be on this journey.

All my career I have been in the people business. Whether I was working in retail, restaurants, or training, the cornerstone was always people. This has impressed upon me the importance of relationships and that you must be hyper aware of everyone you work with, lead, and serve.

Why? Because relationships fuel and inspire the amazing guest service we all seek. Let's face it, leadership is very much about influence and relationships are the lubricant that allows change to happen without too much friction. I'm not naive, so I'd never presume to imply that change can be made easy and painless, but it can be fun and rewarding, even with the pressure, angst, and pain that often comes along with it.

So, let's talk about those relationships. I start here because if you don't have solid relationships with your team, then you are sunk. Conversely, if you take the time to pull your teams in close and embrace their differences then you are well on your way. We will talk more about how to lead this change effort throughout this section, but I want to begin with a grounding in the basics.

You are about to lead a change effort. Whether you need a total customer service overhaul or if you are just fine tuning the overall operation, there will be change. Change can be scary as well as inspiring, so keep an open mind to drive sustained change.

> *Leaders love to create a spreadsheet or project plan and think their job is done. Obviously if it is on paper, it's a done deal. If we speak to it on a conference call, update meeting, or webinar, then we are well on our way, right? Wrong.*

Leaders love to create a spreadsheet or project plan and think their job is done. Obviously if it is on paper, it's a done deal. If we speak to it on a conference call, update meeting, or webinar, then we are well on our way, right?

Wrong.

Change is fueled by people, so you must keep them engaged and inspired. You must balance helping them feel secure while still igniting the catalyst for change. To do that you'll have to be in the thick of it with your team, working with them shoulder to shoulder. You will need to constantly keep your eyes open for these three types of folks in your organization:

The Believer: This person will back your change whole heartedly; they are a small but powerful portion of your work force. They will jump in with both feet, often be cheerleaders for the initiative, and work tirelessly on your change effort. However, they may not be helpful about finding potential pitfalls with the change. Sometimes those who blindly follow can be as dangerous as those who balk at everything. Keep them up front to be great promoters and harness their fantastic energy, but don't buy into their enthusiasm wholly. They will convince you to read your own press and become way too enamored with your change effort (leading to blind spots in your leadership). These folks, however, can be your key change agents and your early adopters. They will be important as you develop and test strategies – and determine benchmarking for what is working and what is not. While they will be willing to go first and test new processes, they will need prodding to give you the dirt on what might not be working.

The Maintainer: This person wants things the way they have always been, or maybe they want the change if it's easier. Maybe they just want a Twinkie ® from the vending machine. That's right, they are your wafflers, your undecided, and your uncommitted teammates. They are likely to lay back and do what is easiest and will not necessarily get in the way (but they won't be a huge help either). They are waiting to see whether change or status quo ultimately wins. The trick here is to bring them along, as their loyalties are there for the picking. Convince them. Motivate them. Inspire them. If you can get them pulling the rope in your direction, they will be a powerful force. It is no small order but show them what's in it for them when the change wins – more efficient work, better conditions, improved hours – and you may find them buying in eventually.

The Disbeliever: This person will be very easy to find. Actually, they'll find you. Every minute of every day, they will let you know how doomed the effort it. Some of these folks will actively try to block the change and others will be paralyzed with fear. The effect is the same – an infectious type of poison that if left unchecked, will kill your change effort. You must give them a generous amount of time to discuss their concerns and then work to convince them. I'm not going to sugar coat this – many will never be converted. For some you will just have to settle for them not getting in the way or sowing discontent. You may even have to discipline or let some of these folks go through the process, but don't disregard anything that they have to say. They will definitely give you plenty to think about, including dangers you may not have considered. They will let you know about gaps in training, technology, or infrastructure that may derail your cause. Fixing these will keep your change alive and perhaps begin to bring some of these folks over to your cause.

As you identify the players in your change effort, you'll need to make sure you craft a plan to keep everyone moving in the same direction. Customer service is a contact sport that demands the best of us every day to deliver the experiences our guests seek.

First, you must start by identifying your change:

To deliver amazing experiences that delight and amaze with consistency and daily magic.

Next:

List the training activities and resources needed to make the change a reality.

Finally:

Marshall the resources and personnel that are required to move from your current state to your desired state.

As you implement your plans to deliver the best in service and experience, you will need to:

Ask for Thoughts About the Change Effort but Keep the Goal in Mind:

It is easy to believe that you have the very best idea in the world but if you don't allow for input from the team and make sure you have buy-in you may fail. You can unilaterally declare policy and mandate adherence but while you might see short term success it won't last. The more involved the front-line team feels then the more likely they will be the change agents that will help you move your plan forward. Be reasonable. Listen to their ideas then plot a course. Be open to divergent points of view and if you hear something worth adding or integrating into your plan, great. If not, don't be swayed. Unless you have compelling reasons to make changes, have faith in your plan and inspire your team to get on board.

Discuss with the Team the Best Way to Implement the Change:

As a leader you may have a great global view on the organization and the need for amazing customer service, but you will need the team to find the best way to implement. After you have taken the time to share your vision with the team, this is a great time to enlist their help with implementation. Chances are they are already aware of the issues you seek to solve and likely have great ideas to address those problems to make your change effort a success.

Be Clear and Open About the Change and What It Means:

This will build trust about the change effort and keep rumor mongering from derailing your process. This means being transparent about goals and the amount of work expected from the team to achieve the goals. If you don't take the time to honestly share the objective and why it is important, you'll give plenty of grist to the rumor mill – and that is the last thing you need in the middle of a change effort. Your best bet here is to own the process by orchestrating the communication and getting the message out the way you want it delivered. This is the way to be sure that any folks who may want to detract from your message never have the chance to derail your plan.

Ask for Feedback Regularly:

You have the goal in mind and a process to drive the change, but there will be many changes to the plan along the way. Hardly ever does a major change effort happen without hiccups and a need to readjust the strategy a bit. Think of it this way – if you are driving from Chicago to Orlando, you have a route planned but you won't know about last minute road closures, traffic accidents, and gridlock. You have a pretty good idea that things like this could happen and that you could run into these issues, but the specifics won't be known until you run upon them (or until your phone GPS pings you). The same is true with change. You certainly know there will be obstacles but who and what they might be will be invisible until they occur. Just like the car trip analogy, you probably have a good idea of potential choke points just like you know you might hit traffic in Atlanta, but you'll deal with it when you get there. So, it's important not to get bogged down with what could go wrong, but at the same time be ready to adjust and have a backup plan in mind.

Celebrate Successes and Give Away Credit Enthusiastically:

There is nothing better than feeling good about a job well done. We will discuss praise more thoroughly later, but it is critical to drive results. If you ask your team to execute this fantastic change for your guests and business then fail to recognize their successes, you'll have a hard time getting them to help you again. Remember, as the leader, you win when the change works, so give away the praise to those who made the change successful. You're not an individual contributor who rebranded the web site, the marketing pieces, or the training program, but rather the person whose vision set the path. Energize your team by making sure they feel appreciated and that others in the organization know about their successes. You'll give visibility to those who with great potential and cement your reputation as a leader who develops talent.

Scale the Knowledge:

When you lead a change effort it could be something that impacts your department or a large organization. The good news is that you will learn lessons that you can use on a larger scale later. The ask here is to not only share what you discover with your team but with your network so that everyone can learn. Too often in the past it was thought that keeping this kind of knowledge to yourself would make you more valuable and serve as a source of power. That is old school thinking that weak leaders lean on due to lack of self-confidence. The true measure of a great leader is the openness to share what is learned with everyone for the good of the organization. The best part about this is that it showcases you as a source of meaningful information who knows how to make the most of the learning you discover along the change highway. The next time folks need a change agent or someone who knows how to parlay learning into results, they will call you.

Follow up Consistently to Be Sure That the Team Doesn't Revert to Old Habits:

Some change is sticky by nature. Maybe a new computer program to book hotel stays or a new point of sale system for checking out guests. Others may be procedural items such as how to make a chicken pot pie or clean a carpet. In most cases, something as cut and dry as a new computer program will stick because there isn't much wiggle room there. Things that have latitude, that is to say procedures that require compliance, tend to backslide if they aren't fully baked into the culture, trained, monitored, and enforced. Folks are apt to want to revert to a way that is familiar and, in their minds, easier unless they know that you are not willing to budge on your standards. Customer service is about process and execution, which places it firmly in the second category. Folks can choose to do or not to do it, and you must do everything you can to make sure that your team stays on the path. If you don't, then you will never get the level of service for your guests that you seek. That means training, observing, coaching, and ensuring your team knows that the standards matter and that they can lead to more meaningful experiences for guests.

So, as you can see, change is a big job with big potential. The good news is that keeping the end goal in mind - delighting your guests – will make it easier to paint an image of success for your team.

A passionate vision for success will be a powerful tool on the journey to improve your service and create a culture. It is one of the most rewarding things you'll ever do – to focus your organization's efforts with laser like precision on delivering service that is head-and-shoulders above the competition.

Just remember that the results you achieve will be no better than the sum of your team and the work you put into your vision. A vision on paper with no action or follow up is just a good idea that leads nowhere.

TAKE ACTION:

All change is hard – whether small or large. You must ensure that you paint a compelling vision, share why the change matters, and follow up constantly as the change happens. It is more than a plan or a spreadsheet, true change is a get-your-hands-dirty and push hard type of endeavor.

- Paint a clear and compelling vision about change.

- Explain the reasoning and make sure everyone understands their roles.

- Find your change agents, early adopters, and true believers – these are the heart and soul of the movement from PR perspective. Remember they will buy in fully and quickly, so you need others involved to give you candid feedback as well.

- Follow up. You can't flip a change and then walk away. If you do, you will find that your organization back slides much more quickly than they adopted the change.

- Reward and celebrate those who adopt and find success with the new way forward.

11

. . . .

EMPOWERMENT IS MORE THAN A BUZZ WORD

People love to talk about empowering their teams, but it has to be more than just lip service

I'M REMINDED OF the importance of empowerment when I stay in hotels. I spend a lot of time on the road, staying in a lot of different types of hotels and my standard go-to are Hilton properties. Now I enjoy the Hilton brand and I'm fiercely loyal to them for many reasons that business travelers covet. They're clean, consistent, and have amenities that appeal to me as someone who's on the road 200 days a year.

That said, there are some shortfalls that show that many hotels have not empowered their housekeeping services when it comes to room cleaning. This is not a problem just for Hilton – I've seen this at most hotel chains (I occasionally stay in others such as Wyndham, Marriott, and Hyatt). When I stay at a property that you would consider a chain, often the housekeepers are hesitant to touch personal items. They will leave a half finished cup of coffee that a guest is clearly done with, they ignore a jumble of shoes in the middle of the room, and so on.

The counter point to this are properties such as Ritz-Carlton, Four Seasons, and Disney resorts. Here housekeepers will take a bit more initiative. They will remove that coffee cup, they will line up your shoes, or if your children have stuffed animals, play things, or toys they may arrange them in a playful nature. It is also not uncommon for them to leave extra notes, amenities, or shampoo just because it looks like you need it. For example, when I stay at the Walt Disney World Resort, Mouse-keeping as they're called, always notices that I drink 2 cups of coffee in the morning (and often ask the front desk for more in the afternoon). When they notice this, they take action, and by the second day of my stay, they start leaving more coffee to ensure I don't have to ask for more. Go one step further and a Ritz Carlton property may already have logged in my preference as a coffee lover and upon my check-in I will likely find the requisite number of coffees already waiting without ever having to let anybody know.

So, what's the difference?

What inspires some team members in some organizations to go above and beyond, while others do the bare minimum?

That something is empowerment.

Now empowerment is one of those words that leaders love to use. It makes companies feel as though they are inspiring the next level of employee engagement and that they are sprinting ahead of their competition. But the idea of empowerment is laughable in many organizations.

I can almost hear Inigo Montoya from The Princess Bride in the back of my head: "You keep using that word. I do not think it means what you think it means."

Typically, executives pontificate about the benefits of empowerment while truly not understanding what it takes to achieve it. This is because empowerment has its basis in trust and shared power – something that leaders struggle with across the spectrum of services.

> *Empowerment has one key benefit. You don't have to worry about what is happening when a manager isn't directly supervising teams. The staff have the authority and knowledge to make decisions, thus taking care of guests whether a leader is there or not.*

Empowerment has one key benefit. You don't have to worry about what is happening when a manager isn't directly supervising teams. The staff have the authority and knowledge to make decisions, thus taking care of guests whether a leader is there or not.

Chick-fil-A does a great job empowering their teams. They understand that in the restaurant business – particularly one with a drive through – anything can and does happen. So, they have to be ready to make decision without having to grab a manager every single time, and that became clear to me the day I mis-ordered a burrito in the drive through.

Chick-fil-A has a great breakfast burrito – what's not to love. Scrambled eggs, hash browns, fried chicken, and cheese. I think it may be illegal in 20 states it's so addictive. I remember waking up one morning not too long ago really wanting one of those little beauties and tore off to the local Chick-fil-A with about 10 minutes until the end of breakfast knowing that I'd have to make every light to get my fix.

And I made it...but then I was so pleased with myself that I ordered a sausage burrito instead of chicken. I got to the window, realizing my mistake between there and the call box where I had ordered. When I arrived at the window, I explained my mistake, ordered the right item, and offered to pay for them both since it was obviously my fault. The associate at the window didn't blink an eye. She had them make the correct burrito and handed them both to me without a thought and without consulting anyone.

"Enjoy your extra burrito on us and have a great morning," she said with a smile.

And I did.

Now that was a nifty little piece of service that didn't cost them much, but this is why I tend to gravitate toward Chick-fil-A when I travel and I'm in a hurry. When I travel I tend to be a creature of habit and trust the familiar. My lifetime value to Chick-fil-A is likely to be much higher than my doctor is comfortable with and if they keep up their solid work, they are likely to retain me as a guest.

There are key moves that can drive an empowered team. It's a big process with tremendous potential for impact, so let's break it down into bitesize pieces so it's easier to understand and implement.

You Must Let Go of Some Power:

This is a tough one for some leaders, especially those entrenched in a command and control type of structure. Leaders who aren't prepared to relinquish a bit of authority will find themselves forever needed when it comes to decision making. It's that old conundrum in which leaders who make themselves indispensable end up. They are needed for every little thing and have no one capable of making decisions on their own. This means that things typically go wrong when they aren't around, which lends credence to their thinking that no one can take care of anything important but them. That leads to underperforming or apathetic employees and no runway for those leaders to advance. Why would anyone promote or move them if the place falls apart when they aren't around?

You Must Give Your Team the Tools and Training:

If you are going to empower a team, you have to make sure they know what they are doing. This includes them being well trained in their primary roles and having the tools they need to accomplish their tasks, but also that they understand how to solve problems and what to do in key situations. This is a combination of sharing ideas about what has been done before and talking through potential situations. You can role play with them, discuss case studies, and game out what-if situations. You can begin giving them authority to make decisions while you have leaders on site to help them solve problems in the moment and learn as they go. The important piece here is that you don't leave them to sort things out on their own until they are comfortable, have had a chance to ask questions, and have shown the ability to make sound decisions independently.

You Have to Trust Them:

This is the moment of truth. When you have your teams feeling confident about taking on a bit of decision making, you need to let them try. This involves trust and the potential for poor decisions (which is why so few organizations really empower their teams well). But at some point, you have to allow them to deal with guest concerns or call audibles during the work day when needed and watch the results. You will be amazed at how seriously your team takes this, particularly if you have done a good job training them and letting them know how important they are to the guest experience.

You Have to Coach Them:

You may find that at some point your team makes a bad decision or they go too far with something such as service recovery. If that is the case, then be sure to begin by thanking them for making a decision and trying to care for the guest. This will encourage them to take calculated chances going forward and allow you the opportunity to give them feedback. The feedback, however, can't feel like discipline or you will likely push them into their shell and they may never try to make a decision or solve a problem again. Be forgiving of mistakes but be sure you give them alternatives to try next time. You can make suggestions and float other possible paths after you thank them for making the call.

You Have to Celebrate Them

Recognition matters and what you reward will get repeated. Keep the focus on the positive and make sure that you publicly praise those who put guests first and don't shy away from making a decision. We have a generation of leaders and associates who are too hesitant to make decisions. There is a lot of fearful leadership out there, so anyone who is willing to do the mental calculus and own the decision rights should be encouraged. You are ultimately developing teams who are prepared to take ownership of service and the guest experience – don't create an environment where mistakes have disproportionate consequences.

You may find that some of your team doesn't want to be empowered. You may find in some environments that they shy away from wanting to take the risk and push back on doing things without manager approval. This will take some work on your part to determine if that is a position that can exist without taking on a bit of decision-making authority. If it isn't, then try to determine why they are hesitant. If they have been burned in the past by leaders who were controlling or who disciplined them for making a decision, then you may be able to work with them and build the proper trust to encourage them to try. If it is more along the lines of "that's not my job" or "I don't get paid for that," chances are you'll need to move them out of the organization.

Overall, however, you'll find that your team takes to empowerment to delight guests and bring their own personality to the business. Teams function extremely well when they understand the guidelines but aren't smothered by layers of micromanagement and stuffy rules.

TAKE ACTION:

Empowerment is a key part of building a service culture. The more you grow an empowered work force the less leaders have to be omnipresent to ensure a consistent guest experience.

- Ensure that you have trained your teams well in their job duties.

- Role play what-if situations with your team so you can help them understand how to make decision in certain situations.

- Follow up with your team as they make decisions – celebrate your team for taking ownership and coach them kindly as needed.

- Decide what the best path is for those who are reluctant to take on ownership and empowerment.

12

. . . .

USE YOUR EMOTIONAL WAKE FOR GOOD

Every action you take as a leader prompts a reaction from your team

AS LEADERS OUR teams are always watching us to see how they should behave.

If you have been in leadership for a while, are new to leadership, or recently taken on a larger role in the organization, it's easy to forget that your words have impact. Our role as leaders is to influence teams to work together to deliver a great product, service, or experience. There is a lot coming at employees from organizations, particularly if you work in a large, complex, noisy company. The key is understanding the impact your words have as a leader (sometimes even when you don't mean them to).

So, with that in mind, I challenge you to take a moment and really consider the concept of emotional wake.

I know this sounds like new age gobbledygook, but it is an easy way to think about the impact leaders have after they have left the room. Your team absolutely cares what you think, what you say, and how you behave. In a way, you are the star of your very own reality TV show that focuses around your business.

It is the price of leadership.

> *Your team is watching you throughout the day and judging your actions and decisions. It can frustrate your team and cause chaos in your business if you say one thing, then act in a way that is diametrically opposed to your words.*

Your team is watching you throughout the day and judging your actions and decisions. It can frustrate your team and cause chaos in your business if you say one thing, then act in a way that is diametrically opposed to your words. Teams are more apt to follow leaders who have an authentic leadership style and are truly aware of their influence. This goes beyond formal influence to what you are saying nonverbally through body language, tone of voice, and actions.

I learned this lesson the hard way when I took on a promotion several year's back and moved half way across the country to lead a large team. I had transitioned from one site, ten leaders, and 100 team members to multiple sites, 30 leaders and 500 team members. In my mind, I was still the same guy who went to work, tried to deliver great guest experiences, and lead a team. What I failed to realize is that while I saw myself as the same person I was before I was promoted, the team only knew me in this new, larger role and wanted very much to please the new boss. I was not particularly aware of my impact and learned some hard lessons.

What I learned quickly was to be very cognizant of what I said and how I said it, as even suggestions and thoughts were soon put into action. This led to some spectacular failures and I knew that I had to put the ketchup back in the bottle if we were going to win as a team. These are the three behaviors I adopted to better lead the team, and I believe they are still serving me well to this day.

Remember Your Impact:

There is no getting away from the fact that your words and actions are going to have impact. What you say matters and will influence your team even when you may not want it to. That means that you must keep in mind what you are saying and who is listening when you open your mouth. I often had a bad habit of thinking out loud and that was seen as direction rather than conversation. Also keep in mind that often your "suggestions" or "ideas" will be taken as decisions and lead to action. You can certainly help impact the Runaway Idea Conundrum by putting the next point into practice.

Build a Culture of Sharing Ideas:

Emphasize that you can make mistakes just like the next person, and you want to hear everyone's ideas. Make sure you show that you value your team by listening and asking questions as well as giving them a fair shake. If you dismiss ideas out of hand, folks will clam up quickly and you'll never hear their great thoughts. The good news is that if you listen to ideas and really examine their potential benefit, the ultimate winner will be your customers and clients. There are many ways you can hear ideas, but the most important part is to ensure your team knows you are open to hearing them. You may have regular listening sessions, set aside time in team huddles, or even facilitate regular one on one meetings. As a tickler to get started there is always merit in thinking about things from a stop, start, continue type of approach. This gets folks thinking about what could be done differently and what should be kept the same for the good of the guest.

Be Mindful of What you Say and Do:

You are on stage and in the public eye during your work day. Don't give in to your emotions and always set a good example. This may sound like a lesson in Leadership 101, but we've all had a supervisor who was a complete terror. I think it's a good thing for everyone to have "that boss" during his or her career. It helps you see what terrible leadership can do to a team and inspire you to never act that way. But the point here is that you can set an amazing example for things like customer service simply by modeling the right behaviors. If you want folks to thank guests and smile warmly, you can impact that by showing them how it's done, and that you are serious enough about it to do it yourself. In short, keep your temper in check, watch what you say, and showcase the behaviors you want your team to adopt.

It's important to understand your emotional wake as it is a powerful tool in leading your team. It is a difficult proposition to lead, inspire, and hold a team accountable for amazing service. It takes force of will and a dedication to your guests (and to those who serve them). With all that in mind, you simply don't have enough time to keep doing things repeatedly. If you embrace the impact of your words and deeds, and use them to drive performance and success, you will find that driving change and consistent execution becomes just a bit easier.

It also has the benefit of simplifying things for your team – and a team with a well understood mission is poised to deliver superior experiences.

TAKE ACTION:

Your team is looking to you to set a great example of leadership and service. Everything you say, do, and recognize has impact with your team. As a leader you have the power to set a compelling vision or create chaos in your business with your behaviors and nonverbal communication.

- Are your daily actions in line with what you are asking your team to do?

- What behaviors do you want to model so that your team sees they are important?

- How can you hear your teams' ideas and put them into action?

- Plot a list of ideas on a who, what, when sheet and work through them with your team.

EXECUTIONAL SUCCESS

13

· · · · · · · · · · · · · ·

WHAT IS YOUR INTERNAL BRAND?

*How your team sees your organization
is how your Guests will as well*

SO MUCH OF what we try to communicate with our guests and consumers is all about our brand and how we align with their needs and wants. If we can't make a compelling case that we have something that they can't live without, then what chance do we have of making them long term, high value guests.

Once we have that "something" that they need – a cosmetic, a cheeseburger, or a hammer – and we deliver it with competence and hospitality - we have met their base need. Remember, it's about more than the product and just providing service. That is the price of entry.

It's about building loyalty to your brand and establishing connectivity that creates repeat business, word of mouth endorsements, and incremental sales growth. It becomes much easier to generate new sales and attract new customers when you receive positive social reviews from previous customers.

> *The Neilson Company reported that 92% of customers trusted recommendations from people they knew over advertising.*

The Neilson Company reported that 92% of customers trusted recommendations from people they knew over advertising. That's a powerful number particularly when you consider the megaphone of social media and immediacy of text messaging.

So, creating these types of experiences becomes important to grow aggressive advocates for your brand and that begins by creating those fans within your organization.

There are three organizations that come to mind: Chick-fil-A, Disney, and Raising Canes.

If you aren't familiar with the last one on the list, they are an up and coming chicken chain based out of Baton Rouge, Louisiana. They have a simple menu, cooked to order chicken, and a signature greeting anyone who visits will remember. When you walk in their front door you will quickly be met with a rousing "Welcome to Canes!" This always feels good, because as the chicken landscape (I never thought I'd use that phrase) becomes more and more crowded, service will remain the differentiator. I would also mention that a chain out of Florida called PDQ (People Dedicated to Quality) is one to watch as well because they are mobilizing great service with a next level approach to not just chicken, but sauces and sides as well.

The thing these three companies do very well is to cultivate an engaged customer base. They have guests who not only care about the brand and advocate for it but are partners when it comes to protecting quality. They are invested in the success of these businesses because they want them to continue to succeed. For example, Raising Canes seeks to recruit everyone to be a "Caniac" and Disney wants everyone to show their Disney Side.

That said, Disney does this best of the three in my opinion. They have created a culture where people blog about them, share information together, and give feedback to the parks in ways that shows they are emotionally connected.

I remember sitting on a Walt Disney World bus the first time with my wife as we learned to navigate the transportation and parks. We were asking questions and speaking with families who were seasoned veterans of the resort, trying to soak up all their knowledge during the ride. They filled us in on theme park tips and answered our questions about the dining plan and park hopping. It was like a community and it made learning this enormous destination a little bit easier.

Fast forward a few years and we found ourselves as the old hands on the bus and we were more than happy to pay it forward, as we are now loyal repeat guests who want to see the parks continue to thrive.

Now you are probably thinking that most of this doesn't have much to do with the title of the chapter, but here is the intersection.

None of that would be possible without an engaged work force who strongly believed in their organization. Chick-fil-A does a masterful job by ensuring that they choose just the right leaders to operate their stores, who in turn select great associates to serve guests. Disney has cultivated a reputation of great service and company values, which attracts top talent. Everyone wants Disney on their resume as they are one of the industry leaders in service and branding.

So that leads us to the correlation. You cannot achieve the success of a Chick-fil-A, Canes, Disney, or even Apple to add another, without having a team that believes in your mission and is invested in your success as well.

So how do you do that?

Start by Being Crystal Clear About Your Vision:

You have a vision for your company, division, department, or area. You may not lead an entire company, but you have control over how you communicate the vision to your team. If your business doesn't have a forward-looking vision, then that's the place to start. Remember that this is the place for big thinking but is not the place for meaningless corporate babble. You have to evoke excitement about the future but also makes sure that it gives you the ability to connect tactical supporting actions to get there.

This is where you need to connect your team's task to the organizational purpose. What is the bigger vision above just making the quarterly earnings and growing market share? If you are a restaurant group, you are bringing people together. If you are an airline you are taking people on grand adventures. If you are in the medical field, you are helping people heal and become their best selves. That's the larger purpose. Not every organization is saving the world, but you are certainly making people's lives better one guest at a time.

Communicate well with your team. We will talk more about great communication in several different chapters of this book. It's important to note that one of the biggest gripes team members have with their jobs is that they sometimes feel like they don't know what is going on. If you took the time to create this compelling vision, don't miss out on the chance to tell your team about it. But that doesn't mean drowning them in nonsense. You notice I said communicate well, not communicate until you drown them. This is particularly important when it comes to your frontline team – those closest to your guests. These team members may be the farthest from the center of power (or C-suite), so they often get told what to do, but not why or how.

Engage Your Team Well and They'll Give Better Service:

It floors me that most people know this and yet it remains a big red flag in many businesses. This is because budget constraints often choke out employee recognition events.

The "how" here is simple, but not easy. You first have to commit to keep your employee recognition systems in place and take the time to call out great work. You also must listen when your teams tell you things and take action. You can meet your teams in large meetings or one on one during daily work, but be sure that you take the time to engage with them personally. This is a key place to gauge if your team understands your brand and how they can help customers succeed. It is also a place for them to let you know if they have ideas about how to bring the brand to life and obstacles they may be encountering that prevents them from delivering on the best possible guest experience. You may be thinking: we've talked about this before in previous chapters. Yes. Yes we have. Team engagement is rocket fuel for culture and it must be emphasized within your organization.

Turn Service and Brand Inward:

When you keep in mind that your team are internal customers, this is easier to master. It is your responsibility as a leader to serve your team each day, so think of their experience as well. Consider what your brand stands for and how you ask your team to serve guests, then pose this question: Are we living up to those expectations with our team? If your employees see a brand promise of creating world class experiences, but they can't get the tools they need to do their job, it smacks of disingenuous. If one of your service standards is to thank guests for every purchase, but you never recognize or celebrate team successes, that seems inauthentic. So, ensure that as you work on your engagement and communication strategies that you turn your service standards inward to be sure that you are living up to those same values with your associates. This is a very show-me-don't-tell-me moment that has impact with those on the front line. When they are treated well – shown the same care that you want them to take with guests – it makes it easier for them to provide the level of service that can set your brand apart.

Make Sure That You Market Internally:

If you can't sell your brand to your team, then you have no chance to hook customers. You need to grow the same kind of raving fans of your brand inside your company or department before you can hope to influence your marketplace. If your team doesn't believe in what you are selling and the mission you are trying to accomplish, you will have a much harder time getting there (and no one is going to have any fun doing it). So, take the time to be sure that your team understands the why behind your policies and strategies, and has an active hand in shaping them. Then go after the hearts and minds of those on your team to help them become ambassadors for your company, brand, and reputation. This can be accomplished in a number of different ways but think past posting a sign or sending out an email. These are perfunctory efforts that have minor value, but not much impact. Think about how you talk about your brand to your team, the example you set when interacting with guests, and tie back to stories of customer success when it comes to your brand principles. These have much more impact than a notice on a bulletin board. By all means, do that too if it makes everyone feel better and satisfies your old guard leadership, but go beyond that to find true success.

This isn't something that can take place overnight, but it does have long term benefit if you can accomplish internal branding that is consistent with your external messaging.

There are many tangible benefits, but you'll find the following are amongst the most important.

1. Service levels improve as your team brings a renewed and more positive energy to the guest experience.

2. Your team members are more likely to use their discretionary effort in support of organizational goals rather than working against them.

3. Employee attrition and turnover may decrease, leading to a more tenured workforce with better institutional knowledge and loyalty to your organization.

4. Your team becomes brand ambassadors in the community and their enthusiasm and positive energy will improve your perceived reputation.

TAKE ACTION:

When you align your external brand with your internal brand, you can grow team members who become loyal brand ambassadors in the community. Today's well-informed guest and consumer base is on the lookout for brands that align with their values, and the biggest indicator they have of that is your team members they encounter on the front line.

- Does your team understand their larger purpose?

- Have you helped your team connect their daily tasks to your larger mission?

- What is your brand reputation in the community?

- Does your team understand your brand, and do they know why it matters?

14

. . . .

PROTECTING QUALITY
AND PERCEPTION

What do your details say about your brand?

WHEN YOU THINK about your external brand, it may seem like a large, nebulous concept that is difficult to quantify. It is also one of those buzz words that companies talk about in vagueries that make you wonder if anyone really understands it.

Let's stop for a moment and talk about your brand and what it means. In the last chapter we discussed the brand perception inside your organization. Now we will talk about your external brand awareness.

Your brand is the sum of all the things that impacts your customer's experiences. It is about the feeling that your guests get when they interact with your business and what they remember most about it.

Sure, you have seen brand statements like "Just Do It" (Nike) or "I'm Loving It" (McDonalds), but those are words designed to remind you of the emotion you feel about their products. Nike has a way of making your feel like anything is possible when you interact with their brand. They are about winning, accomplishment, success – and that statement lines up well with that. McDonalds is a slice of America and there when you need your French fry fix. They are present at almost every exit of almost every highway in almost every town in the United States and they are there wherever kids may be screaming in the back seat that they are hungry. I've been there, at that point you are very happy to see the Golden Arches and even happier that they always have a Happy Meal® ready to go.

So how do you protect a brand? More to the point, how do you protect the guest perception of your brand? That is the larger concern.

What's the difference between perception and reality? Often there is a real disconnect between the two.

Think about your time at a retail clothing store. You pick out the perfect clothing items and proceed to the cash register – all the while you've had great help picking out your items, trying them on, and assistance finding your size. They even took the items you didn't want and replaced them to the shelves, allowing you to head straight to the cashier.

But when it's time to pay, you are fifth in line and there is only one person working to ring up guests. There is an issue with a coupon, one person decides they don't want an item, and finally there is an issue with the computer and a manager is nowhere to be found to assist. You look longingly at the two other cashier stations that are not staffed and wonder how much longer it will take. You also begin to think that the business was keen to help shop and select items, but now that you have decided to purchase them, they are less helpful. You think for a moment about putting them back and leaving.

This is called cart abandonment. It happens when an otherwise great shopping experience is marred by an issue right before closing the sale. We will talk more about that in a moment.

But back to our scenario. You may end up staying in line and completing your purchase. Chances are this transaction took less than five minutes but probably felt longer than it was in reality. The issue is that the business didn't look like it was doing everything it could to serve guests quickly. Even if the time was relatively low, the fact that the line looked long and there were registers not in use killed the perception of the transaction.

The disconnect occurs when you, as a guest, complete a survey the next day and give them low marks for service. You might even choose to shop someplace else next time and that can impact the overall success of that business. The challenging part for the business is they will struggle to connect the score to the reality of the guest experience. The clothing business we have been discussing may look at the service they provide and see all the positives – the welcome as guests enter, the assistance they give with style selection, the way they always double and triple check for sizes when a guest can't find what he or she needs. The staff even checks online for alternatives and puts away the items customers try on, but don't purchase. So how can their service get such lackluster marks? Because they didn't watch the entire experience (stay tuned for our later chapter on the guest journey), and that may cost them in the long run.

So now, back to cart abandonment. It happens online when you have to complete a lot of sign up options or in a store when the line is long. You just decide not to buy something, and you figure you'll just get it later (although the reality is that you often won't end up buying that item or you will purchase from an alternate business).

Recently I was online purchasing flowers for delivery on my sister's birthday. I am not much on signing up for loyalty programs for things I don't buy very often. It leads to mailing lists, phone calls, emails and other annoyances I can live without. I remember abandoning an order with one florist that required the creation of a full profile in favor of one I knew allowed for quicker check out. Now this business had the ability to sign up with my full information, but I chose not to do so at that time. They did, however, send me a note a few weeks later thanking me for my purchase and asking me if I'd like to add my full info for easier ordering later. At that moment I had more time and ended up taking the two minutes to do so, mostly because they let me order quickly when I was in a hurry, thanked me for my business, and then showed me the value of adding my full information. Now when I order from them my payment information is stored, and I can reorder items easily.

But when we think about all the things that can impact a brand, they are normally the tactical pieces that customer interact with most often. Don't get fixated on your corporate logo or strategic plan – sure those are important to guide your organization - but you customers honestly don't care all that much. It looks good on letterhead, but a value proposition never served a guest.

When you think about the trifecta of great experiences, it comes down to safety, quality, and service. Guests see these items as both price of entry and differentiator. They expect service to be a non-negotiable item that they can count on and they want to be both satisfied and wowed by service. They not only want polite and competent service, they also want the little extra that makes them feel special. They want your organization to anticipate their needs, know their preferences, and deliver with efficient speed of service.

Quality is the last leg of this stool. Too often businesses kid themselves that great service is enough to keep folks coming back. Other times an organization falls in love with their product line and forgets that service matters. They are not separate activities. They are tied together to create the overall experience, and brands that recognize this are more likely to flourish.

The Apple Store is a great example of this. Thing about walking into one of these locations – if you are an Apple product enthusiast there is surely nothing closer to nirvana. They offer a great product, a compelling environment, and great service. You can book appointments ahead or wander in and wait your turn. If you are waiting or browsing, there are a myriad of things to play with – laptops, drones, headphones, iPads®, and watches.

Everything you never knew you needed all there for the asking, and they make sure most things are available to touch and use. They understand the tactile nature of retail and that if you can get something in a guest's hands, they are more likely to buy it. They also understand that once you've made your purchase you'll want to start using it, so they can check you out anywhere in the store with a handheld device. If you need help setting up your new phone, not to worry, they have you covered in two ways. First, most of Apple's devices are charged so you can use them right out of the box. They recognize that if you clunk down $1,000 for a phone that you don't want to wait 2 hours to charge it. Second, you can get help setting up your phone or downloading your information from your previous model.

This same kind of anticipatory service can work for your business as well. You must take the time to translate into your organization by thinking about what your guests are going to need next. I think about the smoker I put together last summer that included the wrenches I needed to assemble it. Since I travel a lot, I often grab take out meals to eat in my hotel room while I work. When the restaurants remember cutlery and napkins, that makes things easier on me. I also appreciate it when rental car companies include scrapers in their cars during the winter months. I have lamented this often when they have not, and I end up scraping ice from my windshield with a credit card or hotel room keycard.

Remember that culture, execution, and brand trump the superficial elements of your organization.

Remember that culture, execution, and brand trump the superficial elements of your organization.

The best way to ensure that you are executing on these key items is to check them. This may seem rudimentary, but every time you see a dirty floor in a store, a filthy table in a restaurant, or a dust bunny under a hotel room desk that is because someone didn't check. There aren't many shortfalls in a business that aren't avoided simply by ensuring that you are ready to open your doors each day and that you are touring with purpose throughout the day to keep execution tight.

Here is a checklist that may help you begin to identify potential pitfalls when it comes to protecting your brand:

Ideal State	Current State	Resources Needed	Timeline
SAFETY CHECK: No trip or slip hazards, evacuation plan posted, exits clearly marked, team aware of safety standards and practices			
Uniforms clean, crisp, and appropriate			
All team members wearing name badges or other identification			
Guests greeted in a quick and friendly manner upon entering			
No visible cell phones or gum chewing			

Ideal State	Current State	Resources Needed	Timeline
Body language is appropriate— No slouching, leaning, or arms crossed			
Suggestive selling is used to ensure a complete experience and opportunity to grow sales			
Guests are thanked sincerely for their business			
Team members are scripted and well versed in their roles, without sounding stale and rehearsed			

Ideal State	Current State	Resources Needed	Timeline
Leaders can be easily spotted and identified by guests. They are engaging frequently with both guests and team members			
Signage is crisp, professional, and affixed properly. Nothing hand written or dog eared			

This checklist is nothing without the force of will to check in on these items daily. Anyone can create a task list and pencil whip it every shift. The proof comes when you see that the key moves each day are validated by leaders and that validation drives peak performance. There is something about inspecting quality, service, and execution each day and that is how the great businesses separate themselves from their competition.

This is what I call Owning Your Dirt.

This is something that exemplifies good leaders because they understand that checklists and standards are necessary, but they do not, on their own, drive success. Those who deliver the best service have identified the key milestones in the service experience and protect them fiercely.

The adage of Management by Walking Around is a wise one, but make sure that the **W** stands for **Walking** with purpose rather than aimlessly **Wandering**. Too often when leaders walk through their business, they don't keep eyes wide open for items that can really drive quick and noticeable improvement for their guests.

The fact of the matter is that you have to develop those active visual skills to make yourself successful. There is no substitute for the critical eye of a well-developed leader on a well-worn flight plan. As you walk around your business and through your organization, keep an eye on these key pieces of execution. And know that whether guests can see them or not, they matter because they speak to pride and purpose.

Clean Attire is Price of Entry:

Whether you have a standard uniform or simply a policy of business attire, you must keep an eye on excellence here. Make sure that folks are dressed for success, and that doesn't mean expensive. It means professional, neat, and appropriate. If you do have standard attire, then make sure everyone is wearing all the pieces and that they fit well. Please don't consider a name badge beneath you or any member of staff. Wear them with pride and make sure that everyone is in lock step here. This cannot be a front-line associate only mandate. If you want your team to wear them without fail, then leaders must set a good example here as well.

Nothing is Beneath Notice:

Making sure your magazines are not out of date in the waiting room or keeping window sills free of dust is no less important than making sure that your product is amazing and your staff is friendly. Folks may not notice if your windows are clean, but they sure will notice if they are absolutely filthy. Remember that when your guests see deep attention to the tiny details, they will assume that you are paying even greater attention to the big things. If you are in healthcare or running a restaurant, you never want your guests worried about what might be going on behind the scenes. So, keep your plants alive and your parking lot litter free, and they'll assume that all is well throughout the operation.

Stop and Talk to the Team:

It's fine to think that you are super smart, but never believe that you have all the answers. In most cases, leaders spend way too much time doing "fly bys" in their business rather than truly engaging with the team. If you want to solve problems more quickly, take the time to listen to your front-line team members. They have the deepest and most direct connection to your customers, so it stands to reason that they understand their needs best. Take the time here to get to know your team and develop a rapport that will lead to trust. When your team trusts you, they will definitely want to help you win, and that means they'll share all that great information with you. So, stop in the morning and talk to your team. And no that doesn't mean shouting a good morning greeting as you sprint to your office. It won't kill you, and in fact, chances are you'll find that you have some delightful people on your team. Get to know them and let them know you. . . it will be rewarding and informative.

Don't Walk by Problems:

When you are out in your business you are going to find things that need addressing. There are going to be issues to be solved and guests who need a hand. Set a great example by jumping in to help. Not only will this help fuel a sense of respect from your team, but it will make sure that your guests enjoy a great experience. But there is another side to that coin. If you speak passionately about the need for cleanliness and you walk by something in need of a good scrubbing, your credibility is shot. The same is true if you neglect guests, don't wear your name tag, or neglect safety. Good luck getting your team to buy in when they know you don't care enough to set a good example. When you show a deep commitment to your principles and enforce them (even if that means jumping in to take action yourself), your team will respect that and help you pull the rope in that direction. This is also a great time to get your direct reports managers involved as well. Encourage them to lead a walk through your business and listen to what they have to say. Not only will their fresh set of eyes help call attention to items you may have overlooked, but you can help them develop that critical eye we discussed earlier.

Overall, there is no substitute for keeping a watchful eye on your business. Let's face it, most of our front-line team members want to do a great job, but you can't leave the customer experience to chance. It takes the entire team to deliver amazing Customer service, and that means front line associates and leaders working together. Help your team keep a close eye on standards and work to break down any barriers that might be endangering a consistently great experience.

This all ties back to protecting your brand and reputation. The sum of these details will lead to what your customers and consumers refer to as "your brand." That is why execution, service, quality, and safety matter so much – they are the drivers of experience and brand loyalty.

TAKE ACTION:

Checklists themselves cannot deliver great service, but they can identify key pieces of the service experience that must be protected. However, checklists and processes are irrelevant if they are not prioritized, validated, and celebrated by leadership.

- What are the key pieces of the guest experience that must be protected in your business?

- Take time to prepare a checklist – or walk sheet – such as the one above so that everyone in your organization is focusing on the key moves that drive success for guests

- Help your team understand how to execute on each key move and make it clear that you are placing your trust in them to execute.

- Share the key moves that drive success with all levels – your front-line teams need to understand what they are being evaluated upon and what guests expect.

- Don't let any checklist become more important than validating execution live and in person.

- Your brand is the sum of many details – quality, service, safety, and execution.

15
....

LOYALTY: HARD TO INSPIRE AND EASY TO LOSE

Inspiring guest loyalty comes down to emotional connections

I SPENT ABOUT 6 years living in northwest Ohio and I remember vividly when I made the move. The movers finished unloading late in the evening and it was after midnight when we finished unpacking the necessities we needed to function – mostly toilet paper and the coffee pot. It was one of those hectic days that ended with us realizing that we hadn't shopped for a single bit of food for the house and we had a choice between ice cubes in the freezer and that ubiquitous box of baking soda in the refrigerator. We were lucky enough to have family up helping us get settled and it was embarrassing to realize at midnight that we didn't have a thing to serve them.

We were lucky enough to be living in a unique retail space that offered not only great retail shopping but a few well-placed restaurants. One of these, Bar Louie, was a late-night bar and grill type establishment that served until 2:00 a.m. So, at almost 1:00 a.m. on a warm July night, we walked the 3 minutes to the glowing "Kitchen Open Late" sign for a burger and a much needed bourbon. When we walked in after that tough day of moving, we were greeted with a friendly hello and a menu laden with tator tots. The place was still fairly busy for the hour, but the staff was on point and we enjoyed a delicious late-night meal. We were thankful for the generous hours, delicious food, and friendly service. It quickly became a regular hang out for us long after we had grown tired of other eateries in the area. To this day, when I see a Bar Louie around the country as I travel, I often stop in because they are a brand I feel connected to and trust.

That isn't to say that every meal at this location has been perfect. There have been several clunkers when the service dragged, but we shared our comments with the managers there and always gave them another chance. This is because we feel a sense of loyalty to their brand and want them to succeed. This is a common theme for brands like Zappos, USAA, Ritz-Carlton, and Disney. They have deeply loyal customers who are not only loyal, but are brand advocates who want them to be successful.

Let's dissect what can help your organization build loyalty and advocacy with your guests. That is a key to remember. Loyalty isn't just about sales, repeat business, or forgiving the occasional service hiccup (although those are important pieces). The biggest value you glean from loyal guests is advocacy. You gain walking marketing agencies who are willing to tell others about your value, quality, and service.

> *Hubspot reports that 90% of people trust recommendations from family and friends.*

Hubspot reports that 90% of people trust recommendations from family and friends. This makes current customer advocacy one of the most influential and trusted forms of recommendations when potential customers are making decisions.

Building loyalty is very much about first building trust. I spoke with a friend of mine who owns an airplane maintenance company. In a business where someone is going to fly inside your product at several thousand feet at hundreds of miles per hour, you can imagine that trust is a non-negotiable. He told me that there were several businesses like his in the central Florida area that his customers could use and that he wasn't necessarily the cheapest. But he firmly believed that quality and timeliness were the core competencies that kept his customers coming back. He equated this to trust and to value. He provides a service that delivers high quality while remaining competitive with pricing. His clients know what his competition charges, and while they don't necessarily need him to be the cheapest, he can't abuse their loyalty by overcharging them for repairs and parts. So, he continues to cultivate repeat business by ensuring that the planes are repaired quickly and that the pricing remains competitive. He never rushes service so that he can deliver on his safety commitments, but also understands that when someone owns a plane, they want to fly it on the weekends. His customers trust him to hit appropriate timelines and he often works late on Fridays to ensure that he gets the recreational flyers back in the air for their weekend adventures.

Another way to build advocacy is by cultivating a consistent guest experience. Consistency gets a bad rap, sometimes seen as boring. It is true that innovation will often be like catnip to customers, but consistency and a refined experience are winners for the long term. I've always loved technology and jumped on the MP3 and digital music bandwagon early. In the early days of this technology it wasn't uncommon to download music from file sharing sites, but it was normally because you couldn't individually buy songs. Also, at that time MP3 players were clunky and felt more like portable hard drives than anything. Loading them with music was arduous and finding the music once it was onboard was frustrating. I had a Dell model that was fine at the time, but it wasn't until Apple unveiled iTunes and the iPod that music truly became portable. Apple wasn't even close to being first to market, but they did perfect the medium. The interface between computer and player was solid and along the way the experience included the ability to buy songs in a more flexible manner. Steve Jobs found a way to put "1000 songs in your pocket" and delivered on an improved version of the mix tapes some of us grew up with. So while apple didn't invent the MP3 player, they refined the experience and made it something that their customers could rely upon. They created a music experience that just works intuitively and consistently.

Loyalty can further be deepened through the emotional connections you inspire in your guests. There is something visceral that occurs when you take the time to get to know your guests. They love the little things like getting to know their names or favorite orders or something personal about them. This is particularly important if you have "regulars." Think about Norm from Cheers, for example. We tend to gravitate toward what's comfortable and that makes us feel connected to particular people or businesses. I tend to frequent the same local Starbucks quite regularly when I am traveling, and there are 5 or 6 baristas that remember my name and favorite order. That creates a connection that encourages me to want to visit when I'm in a hurry or on the fence about spending even more money on my minor caffeine addiction. With the competition for customer dollars getting fiercer and guest expectations rising, there is a premium on feeling connected to those we partner with and give our business to.

Today's market is complex because of the service dichotomy that exists. On one hand you see people operating in their micro universes, content to interact via technology and exist in a kind of tech bubble. They are, however, very well-informed consumers using the flow of information available to shop, compare, and benchmark industries and particular businesses. So that leads to disconnected guests who are focused on speed, efficiency, and continuing on with their "connected" lives. On the other hand, a portion of your guests want a service experience. They want a face to face interaction with a personal touch. They are looking for human connectivity in a digital world and when they visit your business that's a key measure for them.

The toughest part is that often these are not different people (or personas), but rather the same people looking for different experiences during different parts of the day.

To illustrate this, let's think about a guest dining out. During breakfast and lunch these guests want to order via their phone and have food delivered via a service such as Grub Hub or Uber Eats. However, during dinner time, they may want to have a higher touch experience. They could want to sit down and connect with family, engage with waitstaff, and enjoy a meal at a leisurely pace. They could also be looking to pick up a meal and take it home to create that same experience, but in their pajamas in front of the television. Or in between, companies such as Blue Apron and Freshly have created experiences where you can have food delivered but enjoy some semblance of cooking it yourself. These two services run the gamut when it comes to ready to prepare meals. Blue Apron will deliver a box of ingredients and recipe instructions, allowing you to easily prepare a meal from scratch but without having to worry about shopping or having leftover ingredients. Freshly owns the ground on the other side. The same type of high-quality ingredients and recipes, but with the convenience of heating it up in the microwave like you would a frozen meal. The meals come completely ready to heat and eat for those who don't want to mess around in the kitchen but do want something better than take out.

Loyalty is also affected by how long-term customers are treated. We've all seen the introductory rates for new cell phone contracts or cable television plans. They are certainly compelling for new customers, but they sometimes leave current customers feeling left out and underappreciated. Acquiring new customers is key to growth, but you'll have to work twice as hard if you don't also retain your current customers. These could be large clients or repeat guests in a restaurant, but the principle is the same. The less you increase same store sales, the harder you'll have to work to attract new ones. Also new customers always come with a cost to acquire as well as being less profitable due to inflation and other economic pressures. Often organizations get so fixated on growth that they forget about retention. You should consider things such as loyalty programs and head-starts toward rewards. This may seem like something relegated to your local coffee shop, but rewards come in many sizes. Sure, there are the "collect-10-punches-and-get-a-free-coffee" type perk, but there are also rewards such as dedicated customer support, special call in lines, additional attention from more seasoned account reps, and locked in pricing for a certain period. Today's customers may also look to community involvement and good works to drive loyalty. Can you help sponsor a client's pet charity in some way related to your product? On a more grass roots level, you can have a form of reciprocity for a customer purchase. Bombas, a company which makes socks, uses this as a part of their core strategy. Their website proudly proclaims, "Socks remain the #1 most requested clothing item at homeless shelters. So, for every pair of Bombas you purchase, we donate a pair to someone in need. So far, you've made over ten million small acts of human kindness possible. We can't thank you enough."

They have a rolling counter on their site that shows over 14 million pairs of socks donated at the time I am writing this chapter.

You can also show customers attention long before their contract is over, before renewal is approaching, or when it's time for the start of a new sales cycle. It is painfully transparent to prospects when organizations roll out all the resources to resign a contract when there has been little connectivity with senior leaders to that point. Stay connected with your customers and clients at all levels of the organization so that it never feels like you've disappeared on them. Retention strategies for your customers should be measured in years, not months. This can take the form of face to face meetings, phone calls, emails, and shared thought leadership. The key is that it is more of a drip across time than a flood at the last minute, and is supported by a cross section of leadership in your organization from senior to front line.

Listening to your guests is something that cannot be understated. There is a practice in restaurants called a table touch where chefs and managers visit tables and speak with guests. They ask questions, share a moment of conversation, and then move on. It is a fundamental element of great restaurant management but is only impactful if leaders truly listen. The same is true in any business. You can hear your guests through a variety of channels – live interactions, social media, reviews, emails, surveys, and comment cards. What will set you apart from your competition will be what you do with that data. Our later chapter on Voice of the Guest will dig deeper on this principle.

Finally, customers want to know that you understand how busy they are and respect their time. There is nothing more frustrating than having your time wasted by a business that doesn't understand how precious time is. Think about the hotel that doesn't have enough people working the front desk when you are tired from a long trip and just want to get checked in and head to bed. Think about the delays at the airports when flights run late. These are both frustrating scenarios, and ones that are all too real for frequent travelers.

These are constant reminders to keep waits and delays to a minimum, to be honest about timeframes, and to deliver upon those commitments consistently. That doesn't necessarily mean to under promise and over deliver, however. If you consistently exaggerate cost and time so that you can come in under, that will erode your trust as well. You may find that your customers appreciate you beating the deadline, but also become frustrated because they delayed something on their end expecting a longer wait on the product or service. Think about my friend with the airplane company for a moment. He could always push out the timing for repairing people's airplanes a few extra days so that he never missed a deadline, but he could lose business to others who commit to a more realistic time frame. He could have customers who would have planned a weekend getaway had they known their plane would be ready Friday rather than Monday. In the end they could wonder if he is padding other things (like their bill) or not appreciate the early deliveries because they hadn't planned to be able to take advantage of them.

Loyalty is the foundation for building a successful business. All sales cannot come from new business, so a combination of attracting profitable new customers must also be balanced by retaining those you already have and inspiring them to want to do even more business with you.

Great service and quality leads to trust.

High levels of trust lead to loyalty.

Loyalty is the key to success.

TAKE ACTION:

Consistency is the foundation of trust. When you have guests, who trust your business they are likely to be more loyal and that leads to higher sales. Acquiring new customers is expensive and time consuming, so while you grow your business with new customers you also have to retain the ones you currently have.

- What is the current satisfaction of your clients and customers based on your surveys and comments?

- What benefits do you currently offer for long term and repeat customers?

- What opportunities do you have to expand those benefits, so they feel as valued as your new customers?

- What key pain points are your customer experiencing with your business (or with their marketplace) that you can solve to add value?

16

. . . .

WHEN THINGS GO SIDEWAYS

*If you don't have a plan for service recovery,
you'll only make things worse*

WHEN IT COMES to service recovery, it's easy
to think about it as just fixing a problem. Now make no
mistake, when one of your guests has an issue, fixing it
the most important thing you can do. But it's also important to frame up service recovery as a chance to build
enhanced loyalty.

I talk a lot about my love of certain companies, and
when I find value in a relationship with a brand, I tend to
be fiercely loyal. I don't' give that loyalty away lightly, but
when I do, I am an engaged consumer who looks to say
connected with those brands.

When I travel I gravitate toward Hilton properties. I
don't stay at other brands unless I have no choice, and I
am proud of my Diamond Status.

I find a glass of bourbon relaxing while on the road,

and I particularly enjoy Buffalo Trace. It's a little hard to find sometimes, so I keep track of stores that often keep it on hand and visit those even though there are options closer to my house.

I enjoy vacations that keep me busy, so I end up at Walt Disney World as often as I can, and my wife and I are annual pass holders.

My family discovered Disney later than most. About 10 years ago we went to Disney for our honeymoon and we fell in love with the place. Now that isn't to say that the dozen or so times we've stayed on the property and other hundred times we've been to the parks have all been perfect – far from it. But they have, on balance, been great experiences.

We were tested one day though, on our third annual trek to the happiest place on earth. We had decided to stay at one of the grand hotels and we saved up for some time to be able to swing it. So, we were very excited to be staying at the Contemporary Resort and had high expectations for our vacation. Afterall, when a monorail literally runs through the heart of a hotel, how can you not.

On the very first day, we hit some distinct snags in the magic that made us question if we had given away our loyalty too quickly. The busses ran late, we missed a dining reservation, we experienced some rude cast members when asking for directions, and experienced a very disappointing meal at one of Disney's most signature restaurants at Epcot.

As we walked into the resort at about 10:00 pm my wife and I were discussing if we had given away our loyalty too quickly and if perhaps Las Vegas would be our destination the next year. As we walked through the concourse to our room, we passed the manager on duty and she smiled and asked how our day had been.

"Fine," we said flatly as we passed.

"I'm not buying it," she replied, stopping short just behind us.

"No, really. It's okay."

"I know what a bad Disney day looks like...how about we sit for a minute," she suggested.

And then it was like we were in therapy as we sat down and told her all about our day, in painful detail. She listened, took notes, and promised to follow up. Her name was Veronica and she did a great job of listening to our concerns. The next day we headed back out to the parks, enjoyed a picture-perfect day, and had forgotten mostly about the day before (and all that crazy Las Vegas talk).

But when we got back to our room we were met with a very pleasant surprise. Sometime during the day Veronica had left us a plate of chocolates with a giant white chocolate Mickey Mouse and a hand-written note.

Mr and Mrs Johnson

__I__ want to personally thank you for taking the time to chat with me yesterday about some of your concerns. At Disney's Contemporary Resort, we pride ourselves on being a landmark of innovative design deeply engrained in Disney Heritage.

When I've had a bad day, white chocolate makes me feel better and I hope it makes your day a little bit brighter, too. Please enjoy.

As ambassadors of Disney's Contemporary Resort, all of our cast members wish you the most magical and memorable experience.

Vern

That was a very well-done piece of service recovery. This was followed up by Vern speaking to us when she saw us next and making sure that our vacation had turned the corner into delight.

The nice part about the note and the follow up was the mix of audible and process. The card that was left and the candy that accompanied it were part of a standard service recovery process. The language was 80% stock, but still very effective. The note had a few nuances that made it feel personalized just for us and was also hand signed. Guests love experiences that feels customized or curated just for them.

When I think about service recovery, I think it is about second chances. It's all about a rubber meets the road moment when you can engender loyalty or destroy it. For us, in the example above, solidified our loyalty to the Contemporary Resort. We must save up longer to stay at the property, but for us it is worth it.

So, thinking about the key steps of service recovery, there are a few foundational elements that can help take the sting out of service miscues. Remember the larger your organization, the more likely your Guests are to experience a service issue. It just comes down to numbers. It's great to shoot for perfection, but despite your best efforts guests may experience issues from time to time.

The first key is to ensure that you have a plan and that your team is trained on what to do. They must be empowered to resolve issues and you have to make sure they feel comfortable doing so.

1. Share the framework below

2. Practice in meetings or pre-shift huddles

3. Ensure your team knows they are empowered to fix issues

4. Give them ideas of how to resolve issues

5. Celebrate them when they solve guest issues.

The key moves to great service recovery can be outlined in the LEARN Service Recovery framework.

If a Guest is upset, needs help, or is experiencing issues, these steps can easily be embedded into your team's service strategies. The key is that they understand the steps and will be ready to put them into action so that guest issues are corrected quickly and with minimal manager involvement.

> *When team members can fix issues for customers without having to check with managers, it resonates well and makes the recovery efforts more likely to inspire long term customer loyalty.*

When team members can fix issues for customers without having to check with managers, it resonates well and makes the recovery efforts more likely to inspire long term customer loyalty.

Let's walk through the steps of L.E.A.R.N. Service Recovery.

Listen: Customers often have a lot to say so exercising good active listening skills is important. You may find that they go on and on about what they are upset about, and you may also find that they ramble and even come across as unreasonable and rude. The trick here is to hang in there and listen for the themes in their dissatisfaction. Listening is a skill that we all need to develop and it stretches muscles that we neglect most days, so really dig deep when challenging guests push you.

Empathize: Think about how you would feel if the issue had happened to you. Work with your teams to really think about a time when something had gone wrong for them or a member of their family. When you can truly look at why someone might be upset and how that might affect them, you can begin to see how to best make an issue right for a guest. You must also consider that the issue may be as much perception as reality, so be ready to use your imagination a bit when it comes to understanding a guest issue. When you can imagine how someone may be feeling it makes it much easier to deliver what they may need in all instances of service, not just recovery. Stay tuned for more on empathy in chapter 23.

Apologize: This is the beginning of the resolution. Most guests really want to know that they have been heard and that you are sorry. This is a crucial step that many organizations ruin with excuses and finding ways to make it the customer's fault rather than something that could have been avoided. There are many instances where the customer is absolutely not right, but they are still going to be your customers tomorrow unless you really mess things up for them. So, to the extent possible, dial in on what has specifically inconvenienced them and apologize for that. Avoid making excuses unless you really do need to explain the issue, as guests really don't care why something went wrong, just that you are going to fix it. Also avoid excuses, rationales, or blaming other areas of your organization. Pushing off responsibility on another person or department makes you look petty and unwilling to accept responsibility. Remember that you are the face of the company for this guest and it is up to you to make things right. Blaming shipping on the call center or a policy on your boss might make you feel better but does nothing for the guest.

Resolve: This is where you can be the hero. This is where the magic happens. And tragically, this is where things often go off the rails. If you haven't trained and empowered your team to take action on issues, then this step will consist of them finding their manager and asking them what to do. Guests report that when a front-line team member can resolve an issue quickly and simply, that can be a huge step toward retaining their loyalty. In fact, guests see this as an almost magical experience, even though it stems from a service hiccup.

I have a bit of an Amazon shopping addiction and I ordered a suitcase last year that wasn't quite what I wanted. I was mildly annoyed that I didn't think it quite lived up to the online description, so decided to send it back. I generally have great experiences with Amazon and E-Bags (the maker of the suitcase), but this time was a bit of a miss. Now I didn't listen to my wife and send it back right away; I elected to slide it under the bed and take care of it later. Later ended up being much later (three months, in fact). When I discovered it and realized I was outside the return window, I elected to call Amazon. I entered my phone number in their system, and they called me back within a few minutes. I explained my issue, admitted my stupidity, and waited. I figured it would be a game of telephone (literally) as they shunted me to a supervisor to make the decision. To my surprise, the associate on the phone said he'd issue the return form and I'd see something in a few minutes. I hung up feeling pretty good about the whole thing. I also was pleasantly surprised when the refund hit my bank account about 15 minutes after I dropped the box off at the local UPS store. All in all, a pretty great experience. I became less upset that the bag wasn't what I expected and more impressed with Amazon and E-Bags for making the return easy and flexible.

Be sure your team knows, however, that you are always there for the hand off if needed. You may need to take over if something is outside of their purview (just ensure this is an infrequent occurrence). Or it may be a new issue and they are perplexed by how to resolve it. Never make them feel stupid for asking for help and keep them involved in the resolution process so they can still have some ownership with the guest experience. Finally, if you receive a transferred guest, get the whole story before answering the call or meeting the guest live. Nothing aggravates a customer more than having to repeat himself while trying to get his issue fixed. Each time they repeat the story, they are reliving it and becoming more and more aggravated with your business. Starting off by knowing their story is a great way to make hand offs less painful.

Never Repeat: The final step in great service recovery is to make sure that we don't repeat issues. There is nothing worse than having a crummy service experience, having someone fix it, and then repeat it the next time. We all have that drive thru we'd rather starve than visit because they always mess up our orders. Is anyone else picturing Joe Pesci in Lethal Weapon 2? They always get you in the drive through! When you are training and implementing a service recovery strategy in your organization you have to be sure you inspire not just empowerment, but open communication. You want your team to come to you right away when they have fixed an issue and share the information with you. That makes it easier to learn from the service miscue and not repeat it.

1. You want to be able to celebrate them for fixing the issue

2. You need to be able to scale the knowledge and learn from the mistake

You may find that they didn't quite handle the issue the way you would have but start by thanking them for fixing the problem and making sure the guest was happy. If you jump on them for the issue or the fix, you'll find that they will come to you instead of trying again. It's as scary for them to take a chance fixing the issue as it is for you empowering and trusting them to do so. There is a lot at stake for them when they put themselves out there, so if you make the feedback feel like discipline, they aren't likely to try again. Coach them kindly and directly and make suggestions if you want them to try something different next time. Ask questions about the issue and "5-why" the problem to help them find the root cause. If you aren't familiar with 5-why, you basically ask why something occurred 5 times in a row to find the reason something went sideways.

Why was the customer upset?

They thought their wait was too long.

Why was their wait so long?

We only had one person on the cash register and we were very busy

Why was there only one person on the cash register?

There were two people on break.

Why were two people on break at the same time?

The schedule was done incorrectly.

Why is that?

Frank did the schedule and he is new.

As you drill in, it calls attention to a couple of things:

1. Scheduling needs to be addressed to ensure that there are never two cashiers on break.

2. There is a need for schedule training so that managers understand what to check for.

3. That training should occur for new team members before they make the schedules.

This type of analysis works especially well in manufacturing or anywhere you are trying to stop a defect. This makes sense, since it was first used by Toyota. You may also hear this called a fishbone diagram as well.

Success here requires that you dig to the root cause and don't jump to the conclusion. When you go through this process remember that you may arrive at several causal elements, not just one. So be prepared to discover several items you may need to correct to keep the issues from recurring.

The overall implementation of service recovery will take time and requires trust with leaders and team members. Discuss with your team and ensure that they know the process and are empowered to make things right for guests. Often the issue will be simple things like a cold food item, product that didn't meet their expectations, or a long wait for a service. Role play with your teams and ensure they understand how to resolve the most prevalent issues quickly and with care.

The key here is to push for flawless service each day, while understanding that the larger your business is, the greater number of guests you serve, and the more opportunities there are for service that falls short. Large companies understand that along the journey to perfection there will be some potholes to navigate. So, take a leaf out of their playbook and be prepared. Ensure your team knows the steps to resolve issues and that if they need help, you are always there to assist.

As you build this level of trust, the ultimate beneficiary will be the guest. She will never suffer more than is necessary when things go wrong and ultimately, she will still leave happy, satisfied, and loyal.

TAKE ACTION:

The larger your organization, the more likely you are going to have service or execution issues. Understanding that despite everyone's best efforts, sometimes things don't go quite as planned can help your team not panic and handle service recovery in a way that still builds guest loyalty

- Help your team understand what great execution looks like and where quality or service could potentially go astray.

- Discuss what the team can do when it comes to handling guest issues. Give them ideas and share examples of what has worked in the past.

- Practice the steps of service recovery in meetings and pre-shift huddles.

- Empower your teams to solve as much as possible and to brief you afterwards.

- Let them know that you are available if needed.

- Recognize and celebrate team members who resolve issues well.

- Learn from service opportunities so that they aren't repeated.

17

....

MANAGING DIGITAL

Virtual experiences are about convenience,
but still center on people

DIGITAL IS THE newest (but not new) landscape
that guest experience must address. As experiences have
gone online and in-app, it's another piece of service that
businesses must address if they are to cultivate a loyal
following.

My first foray into online ordering was for hard
goods at Amazon. These days I can hardly remember a
time when I couldn't pick up my phone and order whatever I need.

Most recently I had an amazing Omnichannel experience with a drone company called DJI. I never knew
I needed a drone and honestly never thought I could fly
one. I was always worried about crashing it, losing it, or
flying it where I wasn't supposed to. I just saw a story
on a morning news show a few days ago about a drone
that shut down Newark Airport for several hours. I never
wanted to be in that position.

But my brother-in-law convinced me that it would be a great thing for my YouTube channel and that I could use it like a virtual cameraman. So, I started doing the research. After a few hours of knocking about on DJI's website, I had watched all their videos and read much of their materials and still had a few questions. I picked up the phone and called them. They answered my questions and took great care of me while I was on the phone with them.

Lose it? It has a return to home feature locked in by GPS. If it loses signal or if you push a button it just comes back.

Crash it? There is some serious tech involved in today's drones that helps them avoid obstacles (aka the ground and trees).

Fly it where you aren't supposed to fly it? No way. The drone comes with built in geo system that lets you know when you are in restricted space and won't even take off in a no-fly zone.

Later when I had an issue activating the drone, I was able to email them for a little how-to assistance. And as I became more and more experienced, I continued to watch their new videos about upcoming products, new features, and tips to make the most of the equipment. Between their website, community forums, and YouTube channel, the experience for me as a pilot and consumer is seamless and easy.

> *This is what customers are looking for −a connected experience that all fits together.*

This is what customers are looking for −a connected experience that all fits together.

Think about digital as just another part of the customer experience, not one that needs to be considered apart from other areas. Think about how social media, phone, and web all can support each other to inform customers and deliver effective service.

Start by challenging IT to think about the guest experience. This means having them use their IT skills to make technology simple. Often the tech team can easily get distracted by innovative solutions without considering whether they work for guests. This also goes for the team that manages your internal information technology. How often do your IT professionals seem like they are anything but service oriented, and often this is because they don't do well at explaining things to non tech people in a way they can understand. IT teams need to keep customer service (both internal and external) top of mind to ensure good experiences for all. The tech needs to work and be easy to use - after that they can worry about anything extra. This can be accomplished by looking at systems from the customer point of view for ease of use and functionality. Consider how customers will use the system and what part of their journey they may be looking to satisfy. This is key as you organize your online tools in relevant ways for customers. Be sure to position self-service, ordering, or finding help depending on the importance to your audience.

Ask yourself "What does omnichannel mean to my business?" We talk more about the omnichannel experience within the guest journey chapter, but you must consider it as a part of digital. Never forget to look at how phone, email, social, live support, apps, and brick and mortar all fit together. That is the true meaning of delivering a great omnichannel experience. Do your platforms offer an integrated experience that aligns goals, messaging, branding, and support?

The human touch still matters when it comes to service. Whether it's the touches on the website that consider how people use technology or the associate who picks up the online chat to offer assistance, people still drive service. It's also important to note that you can set yourself apart by making it easy to find a live person – mostly because many websites seem to make it a scavenger hunt to find a phone number for live help. The other piece to consider is mobile ordering or pick up. I think about Kroger and their Clicklist® ordering system. You select your groceries on their app, select a pick up time, and show up within an hour window to collect your Spam. The best part is that you don' have to get out of your car on a cold day. The associate knocks on your window, confirms your name and order, alerts you of out of stocks, then loads your groceries in your trunk. He or she thanks you and wishes you a great day and off you go. It's pretty well done, and the associates are usually very nice and expeditious. The other app I use a lot is the Starbucks app, as its great for cutting the line. I order from the parking lot and then walk in and collect my drink, not having to talk to anyone. Now that's the scary part (and why incidental greetings are so important). On one occasion, the only contact I had was with two associates I crossed paths with as I entered and exited the store. One smiled and said hello and the other just walked by. Think about the risk here. The only chance they had to build a personal connection with me in the store was when I crossed paths with the team, and they only had a 50% success rate. This is better than many retail establishments and why training your team to smile and say hello to as many folks as possible is so important. The more people you have working to engage guests, the greater the likelihood someone will have a connected moment with one of your team.

Data ethics and protection will continue to be a topic of conversation for some time to come. Whether it's what you hear in the news about social media platforms selling your data or a credit card breach at an online retailer, your customers want to know that their data is secure. Showing transparency, ethics, and security when it comes to online data is something all organizations will have to answer to in the foreseeable future. Make sure your processes are locked down and your security is tight. This is the boring minutia that makes all the difference. Payment Card Industry (PCI) compliance is a big deal here and has to do with how you handle credit card data. You also need to consider network security, protection of your gift card assets, and of course, personal information. Data is a valuable commodity and privacy is always a chief concern to your customers. Whether you are dealing with HIPPA concerns or protecting financial data, you must meet this challenge with resources and accountability.

Chatbots are something you need to consider. Most times you can spot them, but they are getting better. Whether they are pinging you on a travel website to see if you need help or gathering data from you while waiting for a live associate to free up and take over, they are more prevalent each day. This form of Artificial Intelligence (A.I.) will continue to be a part of the online service landscape so you will need to determine how they fit into your model. They don't sleep or have off days, but they also won't replace live assistance anytime soon. Make sure you utilize them in a way that brings value rather than adding frustration and that your customers never perceive that you are using chatbots to keep them away from live support.

Speed will continue to be a differentiator. Speed of service can be driven through digital service as you make sure that ordering, apps, and social media support guests. By making sure you have a social presence that is monitored and that you offer assistance in real time, you can help customers solve problems and get answers in a fast and effective way. Even older channels such as email require speed when it comes to response. Your customers demand unrealistically fast responses, so be sure you have a system to triage and respond to emails. I find even the automated responses comforting – at least I know that my question has been received and I'll have a response within 48 hours. That lays the groundwork for my expectations and gives me a benchmark for response time. The trick here is to make sure you live up to your committed turnaround.

The digital experience will continue to be an ever-changing environment and one that must balance innovation and common-sense service strategy. It is not a nice-to-have or something that is coming, your guests expect you to have this buttoned up today. Above all it must work and enhance the experience rather than frustrate guests.

TAKE ACTION:

Digital is often seen as a bolt on to traditional service, rather than a way to support customer goals. When considering technology make sure that it is functional and easily used. Make sure that technology remains relevant and innovative, while staying grounded in the basic tenants of great service.

- What is your digital experience from the guest point of view? Have you examined your technology interfaces through the customer lens to evaluate ease of use?

- Are you utilizing chatbots and AI in a way that brings value to the customer experience or just to keep them away from live agents?

- What role are you taking with social media? Are you using it to inform your guests as well as entertain and market to them?

- Are you protecting your customer's data in a reliable and ethical way?

SERVICE
SUCCESS

18

....

IT'S ALL ABOUT PEOPLE

Everything comes down to people.
Those we lead and those we serve.

I REMEMBER A trip to the Walt Disney World Resort about a year ago. I was on a trip doing research for my last book and I took some time to visit Hollywood Studios, one of the four theme parks on property.

Now this is one of my favorite locales, but that night was one of those lackluster nights.

It was raining. In fact, it wasn't just raining, it was pouring.

It literally began raining as soon as I arrived and didn't stop, and not that fun drizzle that feels great on a 90-degree day, but rather that bone soaking torrent that lowers the temperature 20 degrees and smacks of thunder, lightning, and disappointment. So, drenched to the bone I boarded one of the busses back to the Contemporary Resort, tallying it up as a win for mother nature.

But then I got off the bus, found some dry clothes in my room, and headed out in search of a cupcake. There isn't much that can't be saved by a great cupcake.

When I walked into the lobby, it immediately became clear why I love this place. The leaders realized that many families with children had packed it in early and headed back to the resorts. You could tell tensions were running high and family drama was boiling up as parents snapped at children and there were threats of canceling the rest of the vacation echoing through the concourse.

Then he showed up.

It was Peter Pan.

He sauntered in with his handlers and in a single moment everything changed. Vacations were saved. Parents realized they didn't hate their children, and I'm sure somewhere an angel got his wings. Hyperbole aside, the change in the lobby was immediate and palpable.

The families queued up and as Peter crowed at the top of his voice - it was a signal that the rain had no power here.

It was, as trite as it sounds, a little bit of Disney magic.

This was one of those rubber meets the road moments that really can define what a business stands for, and that is where this company eats.

This is a perfect illustration of how small, but significant gestures can make a real difference. And those efforts are the product of people, not companies.

So, when it comes down to it, rarely do organizations, policies, or procedures make a difference at the moment of service. Rarely are they responsible for service magic. Rarely are they the reason why guests give loyalty to one company or another. The reason usually has something to do with the people who make up companies, so let's talk about why that's the case and how you can grow it within your business.

People Are at the Heart of Service:

As mentioned earlier, it isn't organizations that build trust with guests, it's the people who make them up. When you look at the team in this way it makes it easier to connect your team's success to your guest's success. Without your teams – the face of the organization – nothing happens.

People make companies go.

People serve guests, make things, and own the guest experience.

But people are messy. They can be confusing and difficult to motivate, and they take a phenomenal amount of work to keep moving in a productive direction. If you can accomplish that you unleash the unlimited potential and power of your organization.

This is the reason why team engagement and empowerment is so important to delivering a great customer experience. Gallup noted that absenteeism is 41% lower, turnover 24% - 59% lower (depending on the nature of the organization), and sales 20% higher between top and bottom performing companies in the area of engagement.

> *There is a lot riding on an engaged team. As we discussed earlier, not only do they perform better, call off work less, stay longer, and work more safely, but they also are fantastic representatives of your brand in the community.*

There is a lot riding on an engaged team. As we discussed earlier, not only do they perform better, call off work less, stay longer, and work more safely, but they also are fantastic representatives of your brand in the community.

Every team member who works for you has a certain amount of effort they are going to put forward with guests regardless of their relationship with their managers or the organization. They will do so much no matter what and pull back at a certain point no matter what. But there is an in-between, or discretionary effort, that is up for grabs every day. That is the battleground that leaders need to focus on and win if they want to create a culture where guests are center stage.

I grew up a huge baseball fan and Tommy Lasorda was the manager of the Los Angeles Dodgers when I was growing up. He had quite a way with words and I remember a quote from him: "No matter how good you are, you're going to lose one-third of your games. No matter how bad you are you're going to win one-third of your games. It's the other third that makes the difference."

It's the same thing with engagement. You have to get the effort that they may or may not give depending on if you have motivated them, inspired them, rewarded them, and given them purpose.

Here are the steps you can follow to ensure that you maximize their chances for engagement. Engaged team members will deliver better service and be more likely to take action when guests need something beyond the basics or that takes more effort.

Make sure that performance planning and management are not just calendar events, but the way you interact with your team on a regular basis.

I had a boss who told me that my performance appraisal would only be a few minutes because really all he needed was for me to know my raise and sign the document. This made perfect sense to me because we regularly talked about my performance against targets, ambitions, growth activities, and projects for the future. The actual moment of the "performance appraisal" was a perfunctory check the box moment that was easy because twice a month we set aside half an hour to talk about my work. My favorite part about this was we spoke weekly, and sometimes our calls were canceled or moved, but never the calls dealing with my growth or performance.

Do they know their larger purpose? This is something that can't be denied when it comes to importance.

As we discussed in chapter 13 team, members function better and will give more of that discretionary effort if they understand the why behind their tasks. Typically, every work rule and process has a story behind it. I once spoke with a flight attendant and he told me that every item on the preflight checklist was there for a reason. Something had led to an injury, accident, safety risk, or ticked off a passenger, hence why it was on the checklist. When your teams understand their purpose and how what they do translates to customer success, that helps them find the importance in their work. As unemployment ebbs and flows, jobs can't just be about paychecks. Of course, compensation and benefits matter, but a consideration is also the impact that a person can have with their work and the sense of accomplishment that it brings.

Is there a set of promises or commitment that they can look to?

If you look at companies like Disney, Zappos, and Ritz Carlton, they have a shared vision that they expect everyone to live up to. They are more than words, they are a cultural touchstone that inspires everyone in the organization to bring their very best. They normally touch on more than just service. They may talk about innovation, use of resources, candor, teamwork, quality, service, and issue resolution. But don't think that just printing up some fancy cards and posting them on the walls is enough to move a culture, because it is not. But you may find that is a part of the solution. It's a fine idea to be sure that everyone has a card outlining their commitments to the organization and the organization's commitments to them (and even better if it fits in their pocket), but those words are meaningless if they aren't a part of the organizational lexicon. They must be something that's talked about at meetings, used to discuss vision and performance, and they have to be for everyone. If you are going to present vision statements and commitments, remember that they can never be just for the front line, they should be relevant for everyone from the C-Suite to the loading dock. If any part of the organization believes they are not for them then the whole thing falls apart.

You will find developing these is one of the toughest things you'll ever do, and the larger your organization the more difficult it becomes. Start with what you believe as the most important pieces, then iterate the content to get feedback. This is a critical stage but one that can go on endlessly if you don't eventually set a stop point for discussion. This will take some skill as you want to hear the voices at all levels and use the feedback that is most crucial, but it can't go on forever. Then you will need to ensure executive buy in and launch. This will then be an ongoing awareness campaign that must tie everything you do organizationally back to these promises.

1. **Respect creativity and ideas.** No one wants to work for a business where their voice isn't heard and having the courage to be creative and innovative is not respected. Depending on your business, gaining insights and ideas from team members may take on different forms, but be sure that you are hearing your teams when they have something to say. Its fine to set up listening posts or idea exchanges to ensure that things are properly tested prior to being rolled

out to customers, but don't stifle the ability for team members to make mistakes and learn from them. Ideally, mistakes are caught and corrected before they impact guest satisfaction, and above all be sure that key learnings are captured so that everyone can grow from the shared experience. This may sound like freewheeling hippy talk, but there is a solid business case to be made here. Mistakes cost more and tick off more customers the farther down the pipeline they go, so making mistakes quickly and moving on is cost effective and efficient.

2. **Be honest and authentic with your team.** There are going to be times when you have to deliver hard news. It could be about pay raises, layoffs or deferring a bonus. It could be time to have a tough conversation about performance or the future of the business. The best advice here is to be honest, authentic, and kind. There are times when you will be delivering bad news. Do it as kindly and quickly as you can, but never let the message get muddled. Much of performance management is poorly done because managers are scared to give honest, succinct feedback that might sting a little. You should never be hurtful, but you must make sure your message is heard. If there are finances, sales, or customer data to be discussed, give as much data as you can and let people ask questions. Any time there is a perception that you are keeping something from the team or hiding it until it's too late to do anything about it, you'll find engagement slip.

3. **Reward those who build relationships and value service.** When you think about the typical business structure and how team members (and leaders) are rewarded, much of it comes down to profitability and business objectives. These are standards that must be met, since if you aren't profitable, you aren't going to be around very long anyway. But where many see a disconnect in what a company says they value and what they actually value is when it comes to recognition and compensation. If service is important, then that should be a part of the review process also. If your corporate culture says it values engagement, then are you rewarding that? Finally, if you value leadership and opportunities to grow, are you rewarding leaders who grow other's careers and give them new opportunities? Whether it's reasonable or not, team members look to three things when they determine if something is important to a company:

1. Does senior leadership model the behavior?

2. Does senior leadership make it a priority?

3. Is it reflected in performance management and compensation planning?

This is the consummate "put your money where your mouth is" moment and team members are watching to see how the organization will bring what they say they value to life.

These items are particularly important as people form the cornerstone of culture. Most of us will work in businesses and disciplines that can be replicated by the competition. Many can serve a cheeseburger, deliver packages, or sell you a new suit, but people and culture is something that not everyone can replicate. Think about what makes your organization special and how you can grow and scale that into a true culture. It begins with the trust and authenticity we discussed earlier and grows into something amazing that can fuel incredible team loyalty and growth.

When you have a culture that promotes teamwork and longevity, you'll find that your overall service begins to improve. Team members are more likely to go above and beyond, do more with less, and share their great ideas. They will also find ways to be more creative and build bridges to other departments rather than walls that create silos.

Ultimately this leads to agility, engagement, empowerment, and customer success.

TAKE ACTION:

Think about the Disney example at the beginning of the chapter. Much of what happened there was at the discretion of the team members on the ground. How are you working to inspire your team to go above and beyond when it comes to great service? Are you building a culture or a disparate group of employees?

- What is your culture? Do you have one?

- Do you have a shared set of commitments to which all can aspire?

- How will you facilitate open communication with your team?

- Are your performance management events building capability or just check the box events?

19

. . . .

THE STEPS OF
GREAT SERVICE

Consistency isn't a straitjacket

THINK ABOUT WHAT great service means to you.

Really think about it.

Is there a coffeeshop barista who always smiles at you? Is there a bank clerk who always thanks you for your business? Is there a bookstore where the team members anticipate your needs in a way that seems almost magical?

It's likely that if you appreciate this kind of service then your guests will also. If you are a leader of teams and training your staff to deliver great service, turn this question around on them. Challenge them to think about what great service means to them and then inspire them to turn that service around on their guests. This is in the spirit of treating others the way you'd like to be treated.

That's a solid beginning.

> *Taken a step further the challenge is to use*
> *empathy and emotional intelligence to treat other*
> *the way they want to be treated.*

Taken a step further the challenge is to use empathy and emotional intelligence to treat other the way they want to be treated.

This is a great way to begin the journey of keeping the focus right on the guest in front of you. This is also a way to anticipate their needs and deliver the kind of service they are looking for – call it situational service.

There is something special about that moment when we serve guests. Jan Carlzon, who was the CEO of Scandinavian Airlines, called these "moments of truth." These are the moments that define service on a personal level and normally happens between front line team members and the guest.

This is why the front-line cashier, sandwich maker, flight attendant, and desk clerk are routinely seen as the face of every organization. This is both invigorating and terrifying.

What used to keep me awake at night was not normally my business strategy, sales growth, or inventory accuracy, but those front-line interactions. What I worried about was how the front-line team members were treating the guests at 9:00 pm or at 6:00 am. When I ran restaurants for a living, I worried about whether the cashiers who worked for me were thanking guests and if the grill cooks were moving the lines along quickly. I worried about if the housekeeping team was keeping the dining rooms, hallways, and restrooms clean.

That is until we made sure everyone knew 3 very important things:

1. Great service was the expectation
2. There were steps to a great service experience, and they needed to be followed
3. Guest safety and happiness were the primary daily mission

We set to work training our teams and made sure they understood the steps of service that would drive a consistently friendly atmosphere.

The framework we used for engagement at the point of service was the GUEST model:

Greet each guest promptly with a smile

- Every guest deserves an acknowledgement within 3 seconds
- Every guest receives a warm greeting
- Every guest receives a friendly smile

Understand the guest's needs

- Every guest is an individual
- Look at things from the guest point of view
- Use empathy to understand what guests will need and provide it

Elevate service with personalized suggestions

- Anticipate guest needs and ensure they have what they need
- Personalize service for each guest and make suggestions for things they might find helpful
- Find ways to take service to the next level whenever possible and create a little magic

Seek out Guests who need assistance

- Keep an eye out for guests who need help
- Walk guests to what they need whenever possible
- Utilize service recovery when needed to protect the guest experience

Thank them kindly and invite them to return

- Show gratitude to every guest with a thank you
- Offer a farewell and invite them back
- Illicit feedback and share with your manager

We saw improvement relatively quickly, but then we noticed a robotic flavor to the service, which was an improvement from the lackluster service they were providing previously. However, we had gone from fair to good, then stalled.

The reason, as Neo in the Matrix discovered, was choice.

We had given them a set of standards, role played them to death, and then sent them to the front lines. This was so close to being great, but we skipped one important step.

We forgot to let them know that the steps of great service are just a conversation. We taught them the GUEST model but neglected to let them know that once they knew the steps cold, they could riff on them a bit, make them their own, and have a little fun.

Once we included this final step it added a new level of personality to the business and life to service. These steps are about creating a moment with each guest and having a conversation. This goes beyond transaction or interaction to a true human moment. At its base when your team meets a guest, they should be ensuring they know that they are glad they are there, that they have what they need, and that they show gratitude for his or her business.

The steps of service I noted above work wherever you meet a Guest. You could meet a Guest on the phone, walking around your business, in a hallway, or across a counter. The important thing is that your team is trained well in these steps through role playing and reinforcement, and that they take them to heart and embrace the spirit. You will need to observe your teams and give them feedback, rewarding those who are getting it right and coaching those who are not. Bring it to life by sharing stories of great service, and ask your teams to do the same. Then tie back to where those stories align with the steps of service you are training.

There are supporting ideas that go along with the service. Be sure that your team is trained to embrace these elements as well.

> **Safety:** It is really a non-negotiable when it comes to service. Regardless of what industry you work within, there is an expectation that you will keep your guests (and your team) safe. Be sure this is a part of your daily team interactions.

> **Body Language:** Be sure your teams understand the impact of non-verbal communication and the impact of simple moves such as standing up straight, not crossing your arms, staying off of cell phones, and not chewing gum.

> **Respecting Resources:** Whether it be company supplies or time, these are important to our efficiency and our guests' experiences. Teach your teams to respect these resources and make sure that care it taken to preserve consistency and speed of service.

Feel free to design your own steps of service or to use the ones outlined in this chapter, just take care to over-train on these pieces to make it a part of your team's daily work.

TAKE ACTION:

Steps of service are a fundamental part of any team's service delivery. They can, however, lead to rote, mechanical service if not steeped in authenticity. This can be achieved by looking at what the steps of service are trying to accomplish and allowing team members to make them their own.

- Establish your organizational steps of service based on your fundamental guest needs.

- Codify and train them so that your team understands them and feels comfortable. Help them see the conversation you are attempting to inspire with each guest.

- Use role playing to ensure your team becomes adept at using the steps.

- Help them make the steps their own so that they feel authentic and genuine.

20

. . . .

THE GUEST JOURNEY

Everything that touches your guests tells a story about your brand.

EVERYTHING THAT TOUCHES your guests adds up to the total experience, tells a story about your brand, and speaks to what matters to your organization.

It also speaks to them about your attention to detail and the consideration you have given their overall experience.

Many businesses think about their services in a vacuum or in channels, which is counter intuitive to how customers shop, make decisions, or give loyalty. Too many companies, especially large ones, look at the guest experience without regard to internal or external influencers on their customers.

That means that marketing may look at their part to play, logistics may think about how they serve the guest, and R&D may think about how they can improve the lives of their customers. Each one of these departments believe that they have their customer's best interests at heart, but without considering how everything interacts together, they could find that the composite of all these pieces don't necessarily work together when it comes to driving guest satisfaction.

This is where those who protect the customer experience can connect the dots and look at things more holistically. Many organizations try to look at the customer journey or ethnography, but most times that is just executives trying to look clever without really taking the plunge into guest satisfaction. It is lip service designed to sound good but accomplishes little.

This is much the same as the theme of this book. It is fabulous if you know the concepts and even better if you understand the importance, but if you don't put it all together to accomplish something you will never build customer advocacy. Concepts have to move to action and performance.

It begins with the holistic guest experience – a true end to end experience. All of the concepts that follow ensure that the customer is considered during every step and that products are created for them. It matters little what you like or what your organization fancies, because if the guest isn't interested in it then it brings no value. This people-centric approach demands that everything you design is meaningful to guests in a practical and emotional way. Put it another way – don't design program, products, or services that nobody wants or that don't improve the lives of guests.

This also demands that companies understand not just what guests want but how they want those service delivered and how they want to interact with brands. Businesses that look at things from the customer's point of view and design for them in a way that they will utilize and appreciate will find a more engaged customer base. So, this also goes beyond just the product or service you offer. If you intend to implement a new policy, close a location, reorganize your staffing model, or improve internal efficiencies, you must also ask yourself what this will do to the customer experience and value.

There are four key channels that really matter if you want to truly own experience in this holistic way, and they must all work in concert. When they do, you will find increased customer satisfaction, reduced complaints, and less effort needed by customers to achieve their goals.

Journey Mapping

When we talk about journey mapping it is about understanding how customers interact with your brand. You can determine this by conducting interviews, focus groups, questionnaires, reviewing VOC data, observing guests in your business, and using your product or location from the guest point of view.

You can think about the guest's interactions with you before, during, and after the moment of truth. When a guest is in your business making their purchase, it is a small portion of the experience. Of course, there is particular power at the point of purchase where front-line team members meet the guest and serve them, but there is more to the story.

Think about the last time you walked into a quick service restaurant (QSR). You certainly spent a moment with a cashier placing your order, and that is a key moment in the service experience, but there is more that makes up that visit.

Here are a few touchpoints on the Customer journey in a QSR:

- Checking out the menu online or looking for nutritional information in the app.
- Potentially using the app to order take out or to reduce wait time once at the restaurant.
- Driving to the location. Is it easy to get into the parking lot and is there enough parking capacity?
- How clean does the restaurant look upon entering?
- Was the cashier friendly and well groomed?
- Did the credit card machine take a long time to process?
- Is there ice in the soda machine and are all varieties available?
- Does the table wobble?
- Is the food packaging attractive and easy to manage?
- Is the food tasty, the right temperature, and does it look like the photo on the menu board?
- Can the guest find straws and napkins?
- Are the trash cans full?

- Are the glass in the door clean as the guest exits?

These are just a few things which touch a guest as they interact with a brand. Think about your business. When your guests research your brand and look for information about you, is it easy to find and well organized? When they visit you does every touch in your organization serve a purpose and make the guest's life easier?

Retail and restaurants are often excellent examples of managing touchpoints.

Bed, Bath, and Beyond creates a touch-centric environment, encouraging guests to touch towels and linens as they shop. They can feel the weight of knives in their hands or the coolness of a pillow. Whole Foods creates equally warm experiences through food. They have many samples throughout their stores and their hot bar is sensory overload when it comes to smells and colors. Even Costco's sampling on Saturdays has become a cultural phenomenon driving traffic into the aisles.

> *Anywhere along this journey there can be a weak link that potentially dissatisfies your customer and pushes them to one of your competitors.*

Anywhere along this journey there can be a weak link that potentially dissatisfies your customer and pushes them to one of your competitors.

You also want to think about your customers and how they segment out. Think about developing example customers (known as personas) to represent those who frequent your organization. For example, the airline industry may have business travelers, leisure travelers, and those traveling for personal business (but not necessarily vacation). Each of these have different expectations, needs, and wins. Inside of these personas you may also have those who travel frequently and those who rarely travel. Again, each one needs a different level of help.

I fly often, so I don't need a lot of help checking in or finding my way. However, my sister travels occasionally for leisure and may need a bit more help. My sister-in-law, on the other hand, is a seasoned traveler, but often has my two nieces along, which presents another level of need. So, think about who your customers are and what represents success for them at each point along the journey. The point here is to think about everything that touches your guest and if it adds to or detracts from the situation. What are the pain points, questions, and potential improvements to each step of the journey?

Empathy Mapping

Empathy mapping takes those personas we discussed earlier and thinks about how they might be feeling as they interact with your brand. What do they hear, think, feel, see, say, and do? Also, what are their pain points and successes as they interact with your business.

Think about the airline example again. If you are an infrequent traveler, the airport is a complex place. From the point of view of an airline employee or a seasoned traveler, it seems easy enough to navigate, but that is because experience has taught you what to do and not to do. It can make you numb to the pain you experienced when you were less familiar with the nuances of air travel.

To understand what your record locator number is, how to check in at a kiosk, staying under your luggage weight limit, being efficient at the TSA screening area – no one is good at these things at the beginning. But if you don't take a moment to put yourself in the place of a confused first-time air traveler, you could miss chances to help them have a less painful experience.

Empathy mapping, at its core, ensures that you look at things from the emotional vantage point of the customers you serve in a way that helps you to serve them with resonance. The more you learn about them, the more you can treat them the way they want to be treated.

Getting the details right

When you think about end to end customer experience, there are a lot of touch points in your organization. Every tiny detail tells that story about your brand and what matters to your business. When you open for business each day take a moment to evaluate the tiny things that may not show up in your operations manuals. Things like your entry ways being clean, your teams being in professional attire (including name badges), cleanliness, and ambiance should all be considered. What do your guests hear, smell, and see when they enter your locations? Things like dusting, music, and lighting can show your guests that you put intentional thought into everything that touches them.

Omnichannel Experience

Think about this as how your communication and brand channels fit together. Customers have a wealth of ways to communicate with brands and they expect them to all tie together. When you look at your online, live, phone, and chat experiences how do they communicate and work together to serve guests? So this goes beyond a seamless look and feel to functionality and personalization. Keep in mind that if you have a blog your YouTube channel it must support your brand and add value to your customers. How seamlessly is your rewards program embedded into your mobile app? Finally, can you start an order online, finish on the phone, and pick up in a brick and mortar location? Remember it isn't enough that you have these communication channels – if they don't play well together and overall work to reduce guest effort, then they may end up detracting from the overall experience.

As an avid Disney fan, we frequent the parks in Orlando dozens of time a year. One of the nice pieces of service they offer is an omnichannel experience that fits together nicely. You can begin on a website to get information and then either book your trip there or transition to a chat or phone experience to finalize the details. From there your information is available in the "My Disney Experience App" which holds your information for lodging and dining. You can use the app or PC to book rides, shows, and dining reservation. You can use the app to unlock your hotel room door now as well. If you need to talk to someone live, they can access your information at the resorts or parks. If you want to buy photos from one of the rides (like the iconic shot of you going down the falls on Splash Mountain), you can do so at the ride, the app, or the photo store in the park. There are even kiosks if you prefer a larger screen to book rides and experiences scattered around each park. Finally, they have added a mobile ordering piece to their app, which is much like using it for Starbucks or McDonalds. They take your order, you pick a time from the available slots, and then show up at the appointed hour. I have used this several times and find it works very well.

And all these channels talk to one another.

That is truly the key when it comes to omnichannel experience. If you are going to offer the ability to text, email, tweet, chat, or call, then those systems must communicate with one another. If they do not, then what you created to elevate guest experiences will actually become another pain point for them. It can also lead to guests having to repeat themselves, which is not a way to develop loyalty to your brand.

Keep in mind the core message here. There are a lot of ways to hear your customers and look at things from their point of view. You have to take the time to experience your business from their vantage point and then be ready to improve based on what you learn. You must also think about the impact of new policies, services, products, and internal procedures on your customers before making changes.

This will keep you aligned with your customers and they will appreciate that you stay in lock step with their needs and wants throughout their experience with your brand.

TAKE ACTION:

Looking at things from the customer point of view is key if you want to drive loyalty and repeat business. The easier you make things for them, and the more you keep their needs in mind, the more likely they are to develop loyalty and advocacy for your brand.

- When you design products and services, are you doing so with the customer in mind?

- What internal processes or procedures make things easier for the business at the expense of customer ease of use?

- Eliminate any policies that only provide convenience for your business but no benefit to the guest.

- How can your guest interact with you? Are there missing channels? Are you utilizing social and texting to help them get what they need?

- What pain points is your customer experiencing during their touchpoints with your business?

- Place the pain points on a Who, How, What list to determine what touchpoints need improvement, what resources you need to improve, and when you will take action.

21

. . . .

CONNECT EMOTIONALLY,
OR NOT AT ALL

Everything begins by being personal.

THINK ABOUT THAT scene from the Godfather. Pacino is talking to DuVall about a hit and he says "It's not personal. It's strictly business."

When it comes to running the mafia, I suppose that's a fair tactic. But in the world of real business and real people, it's okay for things to be a little bit personal. In fact, today's guests are really looking for those emotional connections.

I grew up loving amusement parks. My family's annual trek to a small park called Indiana Beach is a very happy memory for me. As I grew up, I never lost my love of these kinds of places. I think being someone who has spent most of his life working in high pressure situations and spends more time worrying than should be legal in most states, these kinds of vacation spots offer a distraction that is visceral and overloaded – meaning there is no time to fret about what might be going on back at work.

I believe that, along with the tremendous service they provide, is why I so love Walt Disney World.

It was amazing to share with my son, although he was in those fun teenage years by then, but fun all the same.

But when I think about sharing Disney it is always best through the eyes of the young.

Those are once in lifetime kinds of experiences.

They are rites of passage that don't come with do overs.

For me, just a year or so ago, I had the chance to take my nieces to Walt Disney World for the very first time. With special permission from their parents, we planned the girl's first trip to Magic Kingdom and I wrote this chapter while they were still sleeping off the 13-hour adventure. In fact, the day we took them to Walt Disney World is the day I was inspired to start this book.

The day was pure Disney magic as seen through the eyes of a child, and for those of us who have been to the parks dozens of times, it reminds us why Disney cultivates such great loyalty in their guests.

When the last ride was finished, the final funnel cake eaten, and the last princess visited, all that was left was the monorail ride back to the parking lot. During those few minutes, my oldest niece crawled into my lap to watch the castle grow smaller in the distance, and I asked the obvious question.

"What was your favorite part?" I asked.

"All of it," she replied, smiling through heavy eyes.

I asked again for her most favorite parts.

"Thunder Mountain and being called princess," she finally declared - at this point her nose was pressed to the glass, just making out Cinderella Castle and the Contemporary resort in the distance.

That got me thinking, from her point of view, about how Disney really drives that most amazing loyalty.

I hadn't thought I could be any more loyal to that brand. I place Disney in the same league I place Delta Airlines, Hilton, and Chick-fil-A. Those are brands that I will go out of my way to frequent, even at greater expense or inconvenience than their competitors simply because of the experiences they have given me over the years.

But now, having seen how they treated my nieces, I walked away feeling even more loyal to the Disney brand.

I had forgotten how much it meant to me when they treated my son so well almost 10 years earlier, but he was much older than they were when I took him for the first time, so it was a different kind of experience. There is something more vulnerable about kids when they are 3 and 5 than when they are 13 that it makes you even more grateful when they are treated with respect and deference.

Let's start there. Disney understands that adults will love them even more if they respect their children.

They make a special effort to really understand that every guest is important - not just those paying the bills. The deference that was shown to the girls was outstanding, and my 5-year-old niece noticed that folks all day were calling them princesses.

Making people feel special and treating everyone with respect and dignity has great impact - whether they are your largest customer or new to your organization.

Just because someone isn't your biggest customer doesn't mean that they should have a lesser experience than someone who does larger volume with you. Sure, they might enjoy frequency or volume perks, but they don't deserve a bigger smile or more polite treatment.

Disney also understands the importance of milestone events. One of the neat things they do is their button program. For those who may not be familiar, you can pick up special event buttons at the gift shops around the park to celebrate certain events. You can pick from: "Happily Ever After," "1st Visit," "I'm Celebrating," and "Happy Birthday." I remember pinning the 1st visit button on my son and then again, this visit on my nieces. I was actually celebrating my birthday on this trip, so I was able to enjoy a little of the magic as well. The great part about this is that along with all the other Disney magic in the park, there was the added fun of having folks wish us a happy birthday or ask if they were enjoying their first time in the parks. To watch them smile as they replied "yes" was well worth the price of admission.

Now you may believe that you can't script surprise and delight – the answer is yes and no. You certainly can't script the tales of caring you see in hospitals, but there are some moments you can script. I like to think about the dog biscuits that my local Fifth Third Bank gives out in their drive through. As a customer you likely smile and find it a bit magical that if you go through the drive through with your dog, you're likely to find a treat in the tube along with your cash.

Now, that feels like magic, but there is actually a plan. Think about the process it takes to deliver on that dog biscuit. Someone had to spec a biscuit, find a vendor, and order them for the bank. Someone had to receive them and get them set up at the cashier stations. Finally, the team needed to be trained to hand out the biscuits and keep an eye out for dogs in the cars. A lot of work went into that piece of fun, and the regulars love it.

Engaging your guests at milestone moments is important. This is the organizational equivalent of the free piece of cake we've all enjoyed on our birthdays at restaurants. Knowing enough about your customers to wish them a happy birthday, celebrate their anniversary with your organization, or appreciate their loyalty through a rewards program can help you reinforce your Guests' connection with you.

Airlines, hotels, and coffee shops have long understood that loyalty rewards build a sort of muscle memory that makes it feel weird to do business with a different organization.

Finally, there is the surprise and delight factor. When you think about engendering loyalty with your guests, finding ways to go above and beyond occasionally really helps to cement your place in their hearts. Along with the everyday magic you find in Magic Kingdom, there are some nice touches that are executed daily. One of the newest is based in technology. We were surprised during the It's a Small World ride. As the ride was finishing up a large screen displayed a farewell message and the names of everyone in the boat. This is accomplished by encoding guest bands with enough information to communicate names to terminals. Through geofencing the ride knows where you are and what names to put on the screen. It was a nice touch and something new on a classic attraction.

Ask yourself if you are looking for ways to wow your guests every now and again - an upgrade, thank you note, free shipping, or a surprise mini dessert at the end of a meal are some examples.

> *Often, the smallest things get big attention - such as walking folks to a destination in a retail space, or in the case of our visit to Disney, Cast Members handing out small stickers "just because" throughout the park.*

Often, the smallest things get big attention - such as walking folks to a destination in a retail space, or in the case of our visit to Disney, Cast Members handing out small stickers "just because" throughout the park. People love it when folks go above and beyond, and as long as you have the basics covered, these little gestures mean a lot to your guests.

I really only expected to walk away with stories to share with my family, but instead, there were relevant business lessons to be learned when I spent a Saturday at the Magic Kingdom with my nieces.

- Make People Feel Special
- Celebrate Milestones
- Deliver Surprise and Delight

Keep these three pieces in mind as you work to build the emotional connectivity that leads to loyalty.

TAKE ACTION:

Find ways to emotionally connect with your guests – that could be loyalty programs or through small gestures that show you care. These types of moments make the experience feel personalized just for them and that is meaningful in today's experience economy.

- How can you better know your guests and understand their preferences?

- What pieces of surprise and delight can you script?

- Give your team examples of what kinds of surprise and delight have worked well before. These examples will help them craft their own magical moments with guests.

- Know your customers' and clients' milestone events (such as birthdays and anniversaries) and celebrate them.

- Mobilize technology to help you get to know your guests even better.

22

. . . .

WHAT MAKES A
GREAT EXPERIENCE?

*Great service can only
save bad execution for so long.*

GUESTS LOVE HIP, sexy experiences. They love
to know that a company is bringing them the next big
thing and that they are on the cutting edge.

That makes it Instagram worthy, Snap bait, and
Tweetable.

That is, until something breaks down.

Guests are satisfied by products, but they are loyal
to people and brands. That means that protecting your
reputation is of high importance.

Chipotle learned this in 2015 and 2016 when they
had several instances of food borne illness. Anyone who
has been to the chain knows well that they were a disrup-
tor for several reasons in the dining marketplace. They

practically invented a new kind of dining – this idea of fast casual. That you didn't have to order a frozen burger to get a quick, inexpensive meal was new and innovative.

They became known for responsible, locally sourced products, and an industrial look that struck a different note with diners. They proved you can wait in line and order from an assembly line but walk away with a customized dish that tasted delicious. I am a big fan of them and this model.

Their impact was seen throughout the restaurant business as many hopped on the bandwagon and used this service model. Thanks to the effect of restaurants like Chipotle, Starbucks, and Panera, you can see a bigger focus on the atmosphere and aesthetic at your local fast food eatery. They showed that you didn't need a white table cloth or a full sit-down experience to enjoy tasty, well prepared food. I had lunch in a McDonalds last week that was a huge departure from the McDonalds of my youth. Gone were the plastic seats and garish colors. The tables were wood toned, communal, and more upscale. There were more earth tones and natural materials in use that made the space feel inviting.

But let's get back to execution, because being a disrupter is fun and will get you on the front page for about 15 minutes, but at some point, the rubber has to meet the road and you must deliver for your guests.

Chipotle was all about naturally raised meats, antibiotic free, and fresh ingredients sourced responsibly. They played this up against competitors they portrayed as more old school who sourced frozen rather than fresh items. Until norovirus, hepatitis, E Coli, salmonella, and a data breach all haunted the chain between 2008 and 2016.

Guests can be forgiving until they believe you haven't learned your lesson. Then they will begin to reassess their loyalty. That is what happened to Chipotle. This led to a negative perception by some that hurt their business. Obviously Chipotle cared about safety, but sometimes you must combat perception as well as facts.

Now here is the almost Newtonian nature of the impact. Those who left the chain and chose not to return gave their business back to the old guard. They went back to brands such as Panera, McDonalds, Wendys, Taco Bell, and Subway. They also chose Chipotle's competitors such as Qdoba and Moes. This is according to a Bank of America / Merrill Lynch survey (BOM AML Global research and a February, 2016 article in the The Motley Fool).

But why?

Because the very brands that were perceived as dated and boring had something that the newer brands hadn't quite come to grips with. And that something is process. Those who didn't necessarily want to stop dining out opted for Chipotle's competitors.

Sure, a Bic Mac may not seem very sexy these days in the wake of Kobe beef, free range, locally sourced products, but that supersized supply chain brings something that the smaller, hipper, more nimble brands cannot bring.

The perception of safety and dependability.

A part of providing great service boils down to ensuring that the guest receives the product or experience he or she wants with great care and high quality. Chipotle took a big swing at this perception when they closed all their stores on February 8, 2016 for a few hours for team meetings on food safety. This was a bold step to show their guests that they were committed to food safety.

There are seven pieces to delivering on this promise:

Service:

There is something special about receiving great service. It's one thing to find a commodity or product you like. Think about it, really, many things come down to the idea of a raw item you are seeking. Coffee, clothing, ground beef, hard wood floors – these are food, textiles, and raw materials at their core. So, what sets apart a cup of coffee at Starbucks versus the gas station? What's so different between flooring you buy at Lowes versus online? Why would anyone shop for clothing anywhere but bargain retailers?

It comes down to the service you receive. If you are a master of home improvement, you could shop for raw materials at wholesalers or from the manufacturer, but if you are as inept as I am, you need service and advice (and most likely installation). This makes a location like Lowes preferable.

Urgency:

When you visit a business are they quick to acknowledge you and available to answer questions? Do they know the answers to questions and understand that you could just as easily check online? Many brick and mortar locations will owe their ultimate survival to the ability to be on the spot when needed – think about Best Buy, Barnes and Noble, and Staples. These brands could all be perceived as commodity offerings if they don't provide services and experiences that show an advantage to just going to a website like Amazon or Walmart online to make the purchase.

I am one of those people who agonize over technology purchases and like to touch and play with items before I clunk down my money. I recently stopped into a store to inquire about a laptop and when they couldn't answer my questions about large solid-state hard drives with the memory I needed to edit video, I left and ordered my PC directly from Asus.

> *Train your teams around quick acknowledgements of guests so that they feel value, urgency, and attention.*

Train your teams around quick acknowledgements of guests so that they feel value, urgency, and attention. This can also apply to how quickly you answer your phone, reply to email, or how many clicks it takes to find answers on your website.

Execution:

Guests expect quality along with great service. They don't exist in separate vacuums, but rather service and quality should enhance each other, both being a part of experiences that set businesses apart. This means protecting consistency by following standards and processes to deliver products that customers can count on. When execution and consistency lag, guests start to question their trust in organizations and that could lead to an exodus of business. It used to be popular to say something like "great service can save a bad product, but a great product can't save bad service." I think that is true to some extent, but it can only save a bad product for so long. If the food is always terrible, no restaurant can survive, even with world class service. You may love how friendly they are at a particular hotel, but if the bathrooms are dirty and the TVs never work, it's doubtful you'll frequent that location.

Keep execution in mind throughout your organization and be sure you are validating that quality with continuous improvement efforts and constant testing.

Creating Positive Memories:

Depending on the business you are in, you may have an opportunity to create memories. This is especially true in the service industry. You may find at resorts, restaurants, and vacation destinations you can create family memories that last for a lifetime. You may also find this in airlines, travel companies, and hotels. Most businesses do a fair job of dialing in on service miscues and dealing with them, but if we want to build emotional connections and memories, we need to also ensure that we emphasize the positive with guests as well. This means helping to create memories. When I was working in higher education, my team always looked for chances to take photos for families who were attending graduation. Everyone wants to be in those photos but taking selfies of a large group is sometimes difficult – the families were usually surprised and grateful when we did this.

Occasionally you may have memories or experiences that are not pleasant to begin with. In these circumstances it becomes about lessoning the negative impact. For example, in healthcare, even procedures that may be uncomfortable are measured by the perception during key moments to obtain a rating of the procedure. This matters because those who have more palatable memories of a procedure or process will be more likely to return. You may be wondering how you can possibly make uncomfortable experiences less negative, especially in businesses where you may be giving bad news. Often this is as simple as protecting the privacy of those you are serving. It can also be about making sure that your guest has all the relevant information and it served or helped in a timely manner. Finally, empathizing with guests will help you discover how they might be feeling and how you can make them more comfortable. These small steps can help lessen the negative impact of an unpleasant situation.

Keep up with Changing Expectations:

As I write this section, I am sitting on a Delta flight enjoying a movie while I write. It wasn't that long ago that if you wanted to enjoy a movie or show on a flight that you needed to download a movie onto a tablet or phone. And before that, your only choice was to tune into whatever they were showing on the several screens on the flight and jack into the sound at your seat. There was no choice other than to watch or not to watch. Now everyone has come to see in seat entertainment or the ability to access the entertainment on the plane's network at no charge as a price of entry item. My wife checks before we get on the plane each time and is disappointed if there isn't a screen at her seat. What once was seen as a novelty (almost luxury) item has now become something that is expected.

Some other examples of expectations are wifi in restaurants, backup cameras in cars, and free shipping for online orders. These used to be items that were differentiators in the marketplace, but now are expected.

It is important to balance the innovative with the basics – protecting the overall guest experience and augmenting it with service and consistency. As products become more commoditized, the more service will continue to differentiate your guest experience.

TAKE ACTION:

Driving continuous guest experience success is a dance between innovation and execution. Don't get bogged down in continuous innovation until you have consistent daily excellence dialed in.

- Protect the guest experience by ensuring that your processes support consistent products.

- Validate products and test regularly to ensure quality – if you don't prioritize validation, you'll find that quality slips quickly.

- Innovate in a way to stays true to your brand but adds elements of surprise and delight.

- Remember that what surprised your guests and was perceived as innovative today, may soon be a price of entry expectation.

23

·················

EMPATHIC SERVICE

Connecting with both your team and your guests

WE DISCUSSED EMPATHY mapping within a previous chapter, but let's talk about the importance of empathy in service to deliver upon the guest experience. Some of this correlates back to concepts in previous chapters, because if you want to drive that culture of guest centricity you seek, empathy is the linchpin for success. This is the battleground for loyalty and the core differentiator for team and guest experiences.

When we turn this lens of empathy into the realm of service, it becomes clear how vital it is to deliver a meaningful and rewarding guest experience – one that not only satisfies but builds loyalty. Empathy is at the core of service and when we think about the complexities of modern life, it becomes more relevant as time goes on to create a service culture. This allows us to tailor experiences for guests in a meaningful way – and in some cases to even meet needs they didn't realize they had yet. It often involves the use of imagination (as me mentioned in the service recovery section) to really crawl inside the heads of your guests to understand what they are experiencing or feeling.

I spent many years working in higher education and during that time I watched thousands of students move in and start the next chapter of their lives. I can remember driving onto campus during move in day and watching all the farewells and emotions happening as parents left their students in the charge of the university. This has always framed up for me the importance of understanding what might be happening in the lives of guests to determine what they might need. It is a combination of not just understanding what someone might be thinking, but also what they may be feeling as well. If you weren't present for the farewells you might never know that there is more going on emotionally with these new arrivals than meets the eye. While they may seem composed and at ease, in reality they were churning on the inside.

When students are away from home for the first time there is a multitude of emotions they are feeling. There is the trepidation of something new and the confusion of starting the next chapter of their education. Afterall, college campuses are large, complex places. There is the worry about paying for college and if there will be a job for them after graduation. You throw in the pitfalls of newfound freedom, establishing new friendships, and navigating the complexities of become adults and it's no wonder that they sometimes crack or drop out. I saw so many students overindulge in the freedom and buckle under the pressures that we worked very hard to look for those who needed help throughout their time on campus (especially in the beginning). It became easier when we remembered that the students were someone's loved ones. They were someone's sons, daughters, nieces, nephews, and grandchildren.

This makes it feel even more imperative to take great care of these students and to understand that they may have questions or just need a reassuring smile.

The idea of thinking about how you would feel in their place or if they were your loved ones is a great way to ground yourself to be of service. This is an exercise that many in the medical profession use to better serve patients. They envision a loved one in the hospital bed and think about the kind of care they would want them to receive. It frames up being of service in a deeper way than just understanding rote steps of service or memorizing a list of commitments.

The principles of empathy work two-fold for you as a leader. These are valuable for serving both guests and your team, so be sure you consider how you bring empathy to bear in your team experience as well. As we continue to discuss what it takes to develop a culture that puts guests first, empathy is a key piece of creating that kind of environment. When your team feels that you understand them, they will put more effort into understanding the guests they serve.

When you think about empathy, it is a nebulous concept (sort of like empowerment) that is a little easier to achieve when you break it down into component elements. Dealing with it as an overall concept normally leads to feeling overwhelmed or failing to grasp the key moves that make up true empathy.

Start by Looking at Things from Their Perspective:

A useful exercise to use (and to teach your team) is the idea of looking at things from your guest's point of view. This is something that can be accomplished by taking your team on a walk through the business as if they were a customer. You can have them call into your call center or explore your website, asking all the while if each step is aiding or impeding guests in what they are trying to accomplish. Think about why a customer would visit, call, or seek out your business. What are they really trying to accomplish and how would it feel if there was a breakdown along the way? All the while remember that we never truly know what is going on with a person so that smile you give them, that friendly hello, or that extra moment during a conversation might be exactly what they needed to make their day just a little bit brighter.

Keep in Mind That Every Action Your Guests Take Has a Reason:

You might experience a guest who is having a meltdown in your business or that acts badly during a visit to your location. The first response normally is to get defensive or write them off as a demanding, entitled person. I had an airline gate agent, who is a friend of mine, once tell me a story about a passenger who was behaving badly in line. She told me this person was being loud and belligerent about a flight that was canceled. She said that he was adamant that he get home and that it wasn't an option for him to stay overnight. Many at the gate had just written him off as a business person gone wild and weren't the least bit interested in going the extra mile for him. She didn't know exactly why he was behaving so badly, but she imagined that maybe he had a sick family member or someone at home he was really missing. She knew how she would feel if she needed to get home to that person and she used that frame of mind when she said "Listen, I know you are upset, and I am sure you really need to be home. I'd like to help you so we can just take that breath and be flexible, maybe we can work something out." He did and they found a flight that wasn't ideal but that got him to an alternate airport that night where he could rent a car and drive home within a few hours. Turns out it was his son's birthday and he was nervous that he was going to miss another one. He had committed to his family that he'd be home for the big events since he was on the road so much. I can empathize with that as well as I spend a lot of nights away from home. I get nervous too when flights are delayed, and I'm going to miss valuable days at home if the flight gets canceled.

> *When you think about what might be causing your guests to act out or make unreasonable demands, instead of just writing them off as difficult, you can find yourself poised to deliver service they never expected.*

When you think about what might be causing your guests to act out or make unreasonable demands, instead of just writing them off as difficult, you can find yourself poised to deliver service they never expected.

When it comes to serving guests, often we only use a fraction of our perception to serve. Service has the potential to seem like a bit of magic when you use all your senses to anticipate what customers need. Remember that you can listen to what they have to say, observe their actions and watch for those who need help, and you can ask them questions to gain deeper understanding. The key is to go beyond the surface to get to know your guests as well as possible.

Listen to Understand:

I know that we just finished talking about using all your senses to serve but listening may be the most important one – mainly because many of us fall short here. We are an overstimulated society right now and often something as mundane as listening to another person talk gives our attention span a real work out. We previously discussed listening to your team and listening to job candidates, but we also need to ensure that we listen to our guests.

Or, if staying focused isn't the problem, we are so busy preparing our clever come back that we forget to drink in what the other person is saying. We aren't stars in an Aaron Sorkin drama, so snappy dialogue is not the most important thing. Although, wouldn't we all take a guest spot on the West Wing if it ever came back? I would.

But daydreaming aside, its more about ensuring we get the full message from the person we are communicating with. So, remove distractions (phones, computers, or that squirrel that always distracts you) and really focus on communicating in a relevant way. If you are talking, you aren't learning anything so just let the other person talk and save questions and comments until they are finished. You'll get more credit that you think for being a good listener. You'll be perceived as nicer and more professional.

Now as you work with your teams to better understand guests and serve them with empathy, it becomes important to share stories of service and success. This helps dial in on what the best service looks like and how it feels to make customers happy. Often this sharing will help inspire others to go above and beyond for guests. Make sure your team understands what great service feels like.

You can role play within your staff meetings to bring this to life, read comment cards, and work to help your staff understand the various emotions your teams may be feeling as they interact with your brand. Once they can identify guests who are feeling various emotions, they can quickly move to help them as situations develop.

The seven universal emotions – anger, fear, disgust, contempt, joy, sadness, and surprise – all come with corresponding markers and solutions. Knowing how to recognize these emotions sets your team up to not only anticipate needs but to solve problems for guests when they arise. Emotionally charged situations can be made worse when moods are not anticipated in responses.

Train facial cues and body language to help your team correctly judge situations.

As service and experience evolve, empathy will continue to be an important part of the landscape. As the world becomes busier and more demanding, customers will continue to choose businesses who have their best interests at heart, connect with them on an emotional level, and show they can anticipate their needs.

TAKE ACTION:

Have you thought recently about what your guests need when they visit you and what you can do to make their lives just a little bit easier?

- Think about your guests and what they need – look at your business from their point of view and understand what they are trying to accomplish.

- Make sure your team understands how to empathize with guests and that you share stories of service to keep guests at the center of what they do.

- Recognize that everyone has many things going on in their lives and when we take the time to understand those we serve, it becomes easier to make sure they have what they need.

24

VOICE OF THE GUEST

How will you hear your guests and connect to success?

THERE ARE MANY ways to hear guests in your business and most often the transgression businesses perpetrate is not around hearing guests – it is taking action on what they hear. There is a lot of information floating around out there and harnessing it to enhance the guest experience is the core goal.

Sure, you could say efficiency or growing sales, but typically those are by-products of a well thought out guest engagement strategy. It's important to understand that you make an informal commitment with your customers each time you ask for information. You are asking them to take the time to give you the gift of feedback and if you ignore it, that leaves them feeling a bit jaded toward you.

That old saying "feedback is a gift" used to rile me up when I worked in retail. It doesn't seem like a gift when a guest is kicking your teeth in for a minor issue or overexaggerating the extent of the mistake. But when you can take that dispassionate step back and look at the feedback from a less emotional place, you really can learn from it. Also, there is something good about taking feedback at least a little personally. It means you care and that you are willing to put in the time to correct the issue. It also means that you take pride in the positive comments and use them to springboard to greater success. You can't, however, let feedback consume you. You can't let the bad ruin your day and you can't let the good blind you to improvements that need to be made.

So, stay in tune with these key channels:

Voice of the Customer (VOC):

These are your surveys and some of the most empirical data you'll collect. Likely you are asking questions around experience, technology, quality, and service. You may have your surveys lined up around a 5-point or 10-point scale – these are the most common. You may also ask if they strongly agree, agree, are neutral, and so on rather than assigning points.

One of the most important principles you need to consider is called Net Promotor score (created by Fred Reicheld, Bain & Company, and Satmetrix in 2003). This is a snapshot of those who support and would recommend your business. The question normally goes something like: "Based on your experience how likely would you be to recommend us to a friend or colleague?" This is used to determine how loyal a person is to a business and would they go so far as to advocate for a business or service to someone they know.

If you consider a 10 points scale, you want to focus on the percentage of people who gave you 9s or 10s. They are loyal Guests who will be brand advocates and promote your organization in the community. They tend to spend more and remain customers for longer periods of time.

7s and 8s are satisfied, but not loyal. They are passive and could be swayed by a breakdown in your service or a competitor's offer.

Anything 6 and below is a dissatisfied guest. They may or may not be sharing their dissatisfaction with those in their social circles, but there is a good chance those on the lower end are doing just that.

The key here is to collect as many surveys as possible to create a full outlook on the customer experience and how it can be improved. Follow up, open ended questions can add color to the commentary and allow for deeper understanding. If you can implement a system that allows for that kind of verbatim input, it can help you plot sentiments that are impacting service. You may ask follow ups such as "Why did you rate quality as 'very dissatisfied?'" That can help you directly link cause and effect, making it simpler to implement improvements.

Listening Posts:

Beyond the formal VOC, you may have other feedback mechanisms. You may have comment cards in your business or a place for folks to drop suggestions in a box. Although we live in a marketplace where data should drive decisions, sometimes low-tech methods work well, too.

You can also empower your team to ask follow-up questions and listen well when customers make comments during interactions. They may well hear things that never end up on a comment card or on a survey, so they must be empowered to pass those along to their managers.

The other piece that is useful in some businesses are the direct customer engagements and check ins. This could take the form of a visit from an administrator in a hospital room asking about your care or even the manager of the service department calling you to ask how your brake job went. They aren't as empirical as a formal VOC survey, but they do allow for follow-ups in the moment and understanding the guest attitude in a way that more formal surveys do not.

Social Media:

Most organizations will allow you to post feedback either publicly or privately with them. For example, guests love to take to Twitter to discuss issues they may be having with a brand. If you make it easy and do a good job of following up, you may be able to get most of your customers to use direct messaging (DM) rather than just tagging you in a nasty post. Now some will just do that as a default position because they have grown up communicating in this way, but it does allow for a much larger audience for their issues and your resolution conversations. The sooner you can get the conversation offline, the better you can serve them and the less impact it may have on your business. If you resolve issues quickly and to their satisfaction, often customers will share on social media that you were there for them and made a bad situation great. That can lead to good word of mouth, even though it began as a service or product issue. If you can't resolve the shortfall, the opposite may be true. They may air that in public and try to use the marketplace to get what they want or tarnish your reputation.

> *It's important to collect information from as many sources as possible. The more places and techniques you employ to gather data, the more well-rounded the picture of your service will be.*

It's important to collect information from as many sources as possible. The more places and techniques you employ to gather data, the more well-rounded the picture of your service will be.

As you collect the data and look to put it to use, keep the following in mind:

Stop Asking Guests to Give You 5 (or 10 or whatever):

When you brow beat your guests into giving you great marks, you end up with just that – great marks but no knowledge of how to better serve them. It's great to ask customers to fill out surveys but be careful that you don't get into a situation where team members are asking for great scores.

Bullying guests into giving top marks won't help you improve. You'll just end up with better scores but not improved sales, satisfaction, or retention. I can remember working for a group that had a campaign to ask the guests for top marks as a part of handing out comment cards. The overall scores improved by well over 15%, but sales stayed stagnant and retention didn't improve at all. So, they looked impressive but didn't learn a thing.

Get as Many Surveys as Possible:

As I mentioned earlier, you want as many surveys as you can get. The more you get, the more complete the picture and also the higher your scores will be (generally speaking). Remember that those who are upset or have and axe to grind will always find a way to communicate with you. Those who are happy don't necessarily make the same effort. One of my favorites stories about Harry Truman involves this. He was opening mail one day and he turned to his wife Bess after reading a complaint and said, "why is it only sons of b****** who know how to lick a stamp?"

Be sure you make your survey easy to find, easy to take, and no longer than it needs to be. Your team can suggest guests take a survey and ensure that they offer it everyone, not just those they think will give great scores. Remember that you want to hear the good stuff so you can keep doing it and the not so good so you can take action.

Connect to Resources:

One of the key misses with surveys is that organizations collect data like Scrooge McDuck does gold coins, but they don't put it to work. Survey results are powerful things when they are used to drive results.

- Set goals for your survey results and communicate those all the way to the front-line team
- Communicate daily with everyone how your business is doing against the goals
- Be honest about what guests are saying – good and bad
- Recognize those who are mentioned as service stars and coach those who are mentioned as problematic by your guests. Praise publicly and coach privately.
- Dedicate resources, training, and engagement in areas noted as lagging in guest feedback
- Ask your team for ideas to correct issues that are being mentioned in surveys
- Celebrate the movement of the scores as they improve

Don't Knee Jerk When It Comes to Feedback:

You will hear lots of ideas and suggestions in your surveys. You will undoubtedly be given praise and critique by your Guests. If you are a part of a large organization, you will want to be careful not to move too quickly when you get feedback. Some feedback turns out to be valid and some does not. The point is that you need to look for themes in the feedback, particularly if taking action is expensive or time consuming. If it is a true issue, the data will bear it out and you can validate by live observation and analysis in the business.

Survey Metrics Have to Be a Part of Your Organization's Performance Planning:

You won't see movement on survey results (nor recognition of the importance of them) unless people are measured on them. If you really want to be sure that your business adopts the principles, pays attention, and drives results, ensure that your executive leadership is speaking about them often. This should be bolstered by inclusion in performance planning and reviews. If leaders aren't measured upon them for their rating, increases, or bonuses, they will focus their time on the pieces that are included. Guest experience is too important to financial performance and company reputation not to be a key part of every team member's daily duties and priorities.

Take the time to look at each way you have to hear your guests and work to collate the data into a way that allows for net promoter score and verbatim review. There is helpful information in each of these channels and it can help drive decision making.

When you use your guest feedback to prioritize resources and daily work, it ensures that the organization has the guest in mind each day.

TAKE ACTION:

There are many ways to hear guests, from surveys to comment cards to direct conversations. Taking that feedback and doing something with it will separate you from your competition. Collecting the data is the easy part – using it to drive results is what takes work.

- Are you asking the right questions and does that include a net promoter score question?

- Take the time to share the results with your team and involve them in the process of improving the guest experience.

- Connect what you hear in surveys to the creation of tools, processes, and distribution of resources.

- Are you getting enough survey data submitted and does it represent a cross section of your guest audience?

- Don't push guests into giving great scores. You won't learn anything useful to grow your sales and loyalty.

25

················

PRACTICALLY SPEAKING

A playbook to inspire action

WE HAVE TALKED about the basic tenants of service and experience in the preceding pages. I hope you have found the stories, statistics, theory, and practical ideas useful when it comes to inspiring and delivering a differentiated guest experience. Again, whether you are direct to consumers, serve guests in a store front, or service in a business-to-business capacity, you'll find these strategies will serve you well.

I want to leave you with some additional practical strategies. I have taken over a number of businesses that were struggling with execution, profitability, and service over the years and I have used these key moves to drive a culture of people and service. Most recently when I took over a restaurant group in 2012, I pulled these levers over the course of 36 months to build double digit growth in both guest satisfaction and financial growth.

Here is a list of tactical, practical moves you can make to start impacting the guest and team experience. As we have discussed, the only way to get results is to take what we know works and put it into action.

Just knowing these things is never enough. It's what you do with the knowledge that matters.

1	Talk to your leaders and your front-line associates. Ask them what is working, what isn't working, and if they could change anything what would it be. Plot what you hear on a list and get to work.
2	Hold daily pre-shift meetings or line ups with your team.
3	Review your surveys and comment cards for the past six months and make a list of the top wins and losses with your customers. Share with your team and ask them for ideas. Then take action.
4	Discuss survey results with your team each day or week. Share with them what the goal is, why it matters, and where you are in relation to the goal. Praise the good work and ask for help solving the issues. Involve everyone in moving the needle.

5	Connect recognition to what you want repeated or implemented in your business.
	Take the time to write one thank you note or send one email that makes someone feel special for serving guests well.
6	Make sure your team understands what good service looks like and that you are crystal clear about expectations. This means service training that outlines the behaviors and regular follow ups that reinforce the standards. One and done training is useless.
7	Be visible in your organization and check on things. Too often the reason change efforts fail, quality stalls, and service struggles is because leaders aren't managing in the moment, side by side with their teams.
8	Set a great example. Remember you are on stage all the time as a leader – both with your team and with your guests.
	What you model will get repeated.
9	Put effort into selection. Make sure that you recruit a great team and make sure you (and those who hire) put the time in to get it right. Make it clear that if you don't take the time you'll just be rehiring soon anyway, thus costing you more time and resources.

10	Train your team – it will build culture and executional wins. You may say there is no time or budget for training – so you will have to be creative.

Use micro-training and cross-training to get the job done. If you train five minutes a day, the cumulative effect will still lead to the end goal of a well enabled team.

Finally, remember that there will be things you can control and things that you cannot. You may not have control over your entire organizational strategy, and you may not be able to influence the top executives in your organization. But what you can do is lead the team that reports to you and take great care of those you serve. Make that count.

Wasting time fretting about what you can't control and grousing about the organization won't do you any good – so either make your peace with it or test your hand in another company.

If you stay, be an agent of change and a voice of team empowerment. Understand your role to change the days of those you serve and those you lead for the better and have a little fun doing it. After all, that's why you are in the service game – to take care of people and give them amazing experiences.

Thank you for taking the time to read this book and put your guests at the center of everything you do.

I am grateful you took this journey with me.

Epilogue

SUSTAINING THE CULTURE

This isn't just the flavor of the week

IMPLEMENTING SERVICE IS the easy part. Holding the training, launching the strategy, and pushing out the message is just the first chapter. We have discussed the key moves that can make you an impactful leader in the war for loyalty and the quest for sales growth, and now you have to keep it going.

It falls to you as a leader to help bring this to life every day. Whether you are a front-line team member delivering for guests or a senior leader in a large organization, you have to breathe life into service consistently. You have to set the most amazing example and continue to push for excellence in service.

It is a constant struggle to create strategy in such a way that gives it legs for the long term. But any customer service platform that is to succeed must have the stickiness borne from constant attention, pruning, and rejuvenation.

The challenge when you try to establish and sustain a service culture is ensuring its continued relevance over time. Any program that isn't baked into every piece of the organization will come to be seen as a flavor of the month and not something that folks should rally behind or support.

Ask yourself if your program has a long-term strategy, and if your organization is passionately invested in its continued success. Establishing a Guest-centric culture takes energy, enthusiasm, and a whole lot of sweat equity.

Consider these 5 thoughts to ensure a Customer service culture that will stand the test of time:

Does It Truly Put the Customer at the Center of Everything You Do?

This is the one question that you must ask of each piece of your organization "is this good for the guest?" If it isn't, then you should change or improve the process or initiative. When you are establishing a culture of customer service and engagement, it is crucial that you ensure everyone is speaking the language of service. That means considering the guest and the impact that any changes in policy, execution, or program might have on the overall experience.

Are You Consistently Rolling Out New Tools and Training to Support the Program?

Nothing tells your team that you are committed to a program more than continuing to provide support and

training for that program. That could be by way of training, job aids, or continued recognition for the customer
service mission. If you just roll out a guest engagement
platform and then never revisit or expand the program,
chances are the team will believe that it was a "one and
done" type of operation. Meaning that if they just wait
long enough it will go away or become less important
over time.

Is Your Leadership Team Constantly Reinforcing the Values with Great Behaviors?

Teams will embrace what is most important to their leaders. One thing that can help make great service a part
of your culture is for leadership to embrace those principles. If executives and managers embrace key service
moves such as being nice to guests, engaging with team
members, wearing name tags, and picking up trash, then
the team will see the value and importance in those key
moves. Leaders who adopt a "do as I say and not as I do"
type attitude will find that their teams resist (and perhaps
even actively work against) the change effort. This also
means that support must come from the highest ranks of
your organization to show the support for the customer
experience. They should be talking about it, showing
their support, and tying back to the guest experience
every chance they get. The other complementary effort is
ensuring that recognition is high when it comes to guest
service. Make sure to reward and celebrate those who
demonstrate great service to reinforce those behaviors.

Is Service Infused into Each New Program or Product?

Much like we discussed in point one, service has to be baked into the landscape of your business. You can't have customer service notions that stand apart from your general policies and procedures. Honestly, if you don't begin with that basic premise, then you may well need to reevaluate the overall landscape of your organization. That said, you have to consider all your key constituents. Shareholders, your team, and guests who frequent your business all need to be considered. So, it isn't to say that financial considerations are off the table. But, when you consider things like work force size, productivity, and product selection, you have to balance all those concerned. You have to be financially prudent to ensure the long-term success of your business, after all, you can't serve if you aren't economically viable, but just be sure that you are considering what impact any cost reductions or new programs might have on your service.

Does Everyone Understand Why Service Matters?

Teams who understand the "why" behind customer service are far more likely to provide great experiences. When you make sure team members understand how important they are to the organization and that treating guests well will ensure their continued loyalty, you are setting them up to help pull the rope in the right direction. Today's teams don't function well in silos and without all the key data to make decisions, so be very open with the communication. This is particularly important to the Millennial work force, who thrive on understanding the whole picture and how everything fits together. So be sure you keep communication robust through staff meetings and pre-shift huddles. A well informed, well trained team can help you deliver great service and drive its continued stickiness over time.

As we close our time together remember that this all comes back to the daily moves that drive service. Strategy, checklists, and even this book can't serve guests and drive quality.

Only people can do that.

It takes that special commitment that only those who put guests at the center of everything can provide. Sure, many companies can call themselves "good" when it comes to service, but only a few best in class own the field. Those who find the best success will be the ones who have made the commitment to own it – day by day, hour by hour, shift by shift.

That's the only way it works.

Because together we serve.

About the Author

· · · · · · · · · · · · · · ·

TONY JOHNSON HELPS companies large and small around the world ignite their service and prioritize the guest experience.

Tony is a prolific speaker and guest engagement expert who speaks to thousands each year – from teams of 5 to groups of 500, everyone can benefit from this powerful message of service.

He helps organizations in sectors such as: education, retail, consumer goods, entertainment venues, sporting arenas, restaurants, and healthcare better care for their customers and consumers.

His philosophy is simple: Keep guests center stage and the team well engaged and you'll be rewarded with loyalty and sales growth.

Tony's experiences, strategies, and tactics are fueled by a 20-year career in retail and restaurant groups. He has led large and diverse teams to deliver results, sales growth, guest satisfaction and team engagement. His passion is sharing these winning strategies to organizations on a journey of service.

Tony Johnson, CCXP

WWW.IGNITEYOURSERVICE.COM
Facebook:
/TonyJohnsonCX

Twitter:
@ServiceRecipe

Snapchat:
thetonyjohnson

Instagram:
@recipeforservice

YouTube:
Customer Service Trainer
and Speaker Tony Johnson